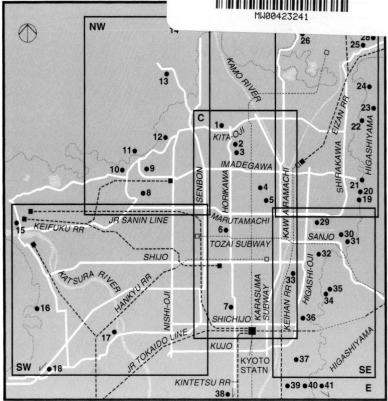

Designed by Marc Treib.

Originally published by Shufunotomo
Company, Ltd., in 1980 under the
title *A Guide to the Gardens of Kyoto*.
Now revised and updated.

Distributed in the United States by
Kodansha America, Inc., and in the
United Kingdom and continental
Europe by Kodansha Europe Ltd.

Published by Kodansha International
Ltd., 17–14 Otowa 1-chome,
Bunkyo-ku, Tokyo 112–8652, and
Kodansha America, Inc.

First edition, 2003
18 17 16 15 14 13 12 11 10 09 08
12 11 10 9 8 7 6 5 4 3

www.kodansha-intl.com

Dedication

in memory of John Brinckerhoff
Jackson, Adjunct Professor of
Landscape Architecture,
University of California, Berkeley,
and Harvard University,
who contributed
immeasurably to our
understanding of the landscape,

and

in memory of Garrett Eckbo,
Professor Emeritus
of Landscape Architecture,
University of California, Berkeley,
who taught us that
landscape design is
a human activity and need not
be a lost art.

Contents

Introduction

A first visit to Japan usually produces both anxiety and excitement. There is a strangeness to the place; it seems different, chaotic—yet exotic. Major cities such as Tokyo or Osaka seem confused—and confusing—and the first-time visitor feels lost. Unlike the American city, Japan offers few gridiron street plans with their convenient "A" Streets and First Avenues. Nor is there a comprehensible, centralized urban pattern like that of the medieval European town. Even products in the store windows look different. The people are different in their form, manners, and dress. Most of all, the language is different, beyond comprehension—strange in its sound and more so in its written form. The city seems charged with meaningless marks, however pretty or intriguing their patterns. And no apparent cognates to words in Western languages comfort us.

However, this distancing from understanding caused by the modern Japanese metropolis is less acutely felt in Japan's historic architecture and gardens, which are certainly more sympathetic in feeling. Their quiet and repose contrast with the density, bustle, and noise of city life. In the historical gardens of Kyoto one slips back centuries to an ordered world of calm and balance. The forms of the temples, and often their layouts, may at first appear curious, but at least their materials —wood, stone, thatch, tile, and plaster—are familiar. The refinement of the forms and the eloquent craftsmanship with which they were made directly appeal to almost all visitors. Yet, beyond this first layer of perception, the meaning of these places remains obscure.

The intentions behind them are not easily deciphered, particularly by those outside the culture. Meaning is often complex, often understated and buried within the form. By American standards, it all just "looks old"; we lack the sense of history that an architecture over a thousand years old and a recorded development of two thousand years can create. The casual visitor will not trouble him- or herself over it. These are beautiful places—that in itself is sufficient to merit a visit and compensate for the time and energy invested in the trip. But to the more serious student, extracting appreciation and understanding from these gardens and temples is no easy task: how can one find the story, know the history, and understand the meaning of these gardens and buildings? Our intention in this guide to the gardens of Kyoto is to present at least a schematic glimpse of the context in which environmental design in Japan has developed, to which garden designers and religious and political figures have made important contributions through the centuries. While it is impossible to paint a complete picture in such a small volume, we hope to at least construct a foundation for greater study.

This book grew from two major

stimuli. First, we wanted to write the book that we wished had existed when *we* first visited Kyoto. Second, we both grew pleasantly tired of numerous, continuous requests by friends, and friends of friends, for our opinions on what to see in Japan; what to see in Kyoto with only three days; and the reasons that it looks the way it does. In teaching Japanese architecture and gardens in the Department of Architecture, University of California, Berkeley, we developed a structure for studying Japanese environmental design as "frozen anthropology," with a particular bias toward those design ideas that would potentially be useful in modern life. From specific instances, a broader understanding can develop. This is not to say we focus on things that could or should be copied as they exist; rather, we address ideas that remain relevant to modern, even Western, existence, although they would, of necessity, take new forms.

We hope that this book is both pragmatic and insightful. This, of course, is a tall order given its diminutive size. On one hand, we felt the need to tell about what is there, when it was made, and when it is open. But we wanted to do more. Most guides are informative or confirmatory— they hint at what to see, but rarely tell why, or what, we can learn from that place. We hope that this guide will provide some direction for understanding the story behind the forms so that the visitor can

learn from our experience.

The guide is divided into two major sections: the essays and the entries. The first essay outlines the history of Japan, politically, aesthetically, and environmentally. The second addresses, more specifically, the environmental history of Kyoto itself—admittedly in a rather express manner—to position the temples, villas, and gardens in the development of the imperial city. Nothing has caused us greater anxiety than writing these essays, the brevity of which forces some sweeping generalizations. And no one is more aware of the problem of generalizing than the authors. We support this approach only because it is often more fruitful to first understand complicated concepts through generalizations, even if exceptions to the statements are certain to exist. We hope that the users of this guide will find a great deal of useful information, and we anticipate that students of the Japanese garden may merely smile and nod knowingly at some of the broad overstatements.

Dating and chronology are another difficult matter. Gardens and buildings have been made, destroyed, rebuilt, modified, moved, changed, and created anew. Each day brings a new garden; nature, like the human being, is never static. When was a garden "made" and by whom? The labyrinth of facts and academic disputes interests the casual visitor (and the authors) only to a point. Even among Japanese scholars of the landscape and architecture there is little concordance. Thus, exact dating and/or attributions for the gardens—if either could ever be firmly established—are not critical for understanding the basic content of this book.

The second part of the guide, the entries, includes the listings of the individual gardens, their histories in outline, and limited descriptions of each. A comments section, where appropriate, suggests the best time of year to visit the garden or a specific aspect of Japanese garden design that is exceptionally well utilized. After visits to several of the key gardens, the visitors should be familiar with the more salient aspects of Japanese garden making and begin to formulate an understanding of how and why the gardens came about.

Of course, the authors do not mean to imply that a visit to the gardens of Kyoto should necessarily be a study tour: certainly, the desired experience is ultimately one of pleasure and enjoyment. But through at least cursory study, much greater understanding and enjoyment are possible than by merely running along the veranda or through the garden to capture the requisite pictures. While a book of this size cannot claim to be definitive in any way, it is our hope that the information presented

can lead to a richer experience of the Japanese garden—which ultimately leads to a greater pleasure and more significant experience.

Marc Treib
Ron Herman

Berkeley, California
December, 1979

_____

A Note to the Revised Edition

Over two decades have passed since we first published this guide to some of the world's most beautiful and moving gardens. The opportunity to see the book again in print is most welcome, but that possibility also raises some basic questions about the best way to proceed. After due consideration, we decided to keep the guide substantially in its original form. Admission and practical information have been updated; the text has been substantially edited and brought into greater accord with our current standards; certain ideas have been developed from those in the first edition. In addition, we have introduced a number of newer photographs to improve the quality of the images. The overwhelmingly positive reception the guide has received over the years convinced us to "leave well enough alone," which we have done—more or less.

M. T.
R. H.

Berkeley
April, 2003

Acknowledgments

We have learned from many people, either through personal contact or through their writings. Günter Nitschke's 1966 seminal article on "*ma*" in *Architectural Design*, has greatly informed our point of view. The insights provided in this article are difficult to escape. Shigemori Mirei's writings have also provided valuable information, as have Itoh Teiji's and Loraine Kuck's publications on Japanese architecture and gardens. Ironically, Japan's early foreign visitors wrote much of the best material on the country's environmental design, and we strongly recommend Edward S. Morse's rewarding book, *Japanese Homes and Their Surroundings*, first published in the late nineteenth century and still an absolute classic. A more complete list of readings appears at the back of the book.

So many people have contributed to the making of this guide that it would be impossible for us to remember, much less thank them all. We do, however, extend thanks to our many friends and colleagues, both Japanese and American, who have aided us in the task of preparation. For help with research, we would like to thank Mitsuo Fujioka of Osaka for garden research. For reviewing portions of the manuscript and offering many helpful suggestions, Louise Cort, Kyoto; Prof. Yasushi Egami, Saitama; Prof. Yoshiaku Shimizu, now at Princeton; the late Prof. Spiro Kostof, Berkeley; and Prof. Henry D. Smith, now in New York. The original publishers at Shufunotomo were most cooperative in allowing us to both write and produce the book, and we wish to thank in particular Mr. Kazuhiko Nagai. Joanna Taylor and Bonnie Loyd helped greatly in putting the original text into comprehensible form. Departures from lucid writing are probably due to the pigheadedness of the authors in their never-ending quest for character in prose.

Particular thanks are due to the Japan Foundation, Tokyo, which funded Ron Herman's study of Edo period gardens during the autumn of 1977. Much information acquired during that period of study has informed the preparation of this book. Also appreciated is the aid of Toshihiro Nakane, formerly at the Imperial Household Agency, Kyoto, for arranging frequent entry to the three imperial villas.

For the revised edition, we need to thank Karen Madsen for critical review and Ayako Akaogi for helping return the book to print.

Although we have solicited many opinions from many people, in the end we must take all the responsibility for not always listening to what they had to say.

A Guide to This Guide

Essays and Photohistory

The book opens with two essays: the first outlines the history of the Japanese garden within its cultural and political context; the second concerns the development of the city of Kyoto, its environmental design, planning, and development. Neither essay is meant to be definitive; each is meant to introduce material expanded in greater detail by the individual entries.

A series of color photographs divides the two essays, presenting selected Kyoto gardens in chronological order. This section not only provides views in color, but also helps the reader trace the development of Japanese garden design through the centuries.

Entries

The largest part of the book contains the individual entries on the most important, and/or accessible, fifty-odd gardens of Kyoto. The sections are ordered geographically, commencing with Central Kyoto, and then moving outwards in a loosely spiral manner, presenting next the Northwest, Southwest, Northeast, Southeast, and ending with the Environs of Kyoto, that is, outside Kyoto proper. The heading for each entry lists the name of the garden or temple in bold type, followed by the period and date of its founding (if known), its religious sect where appropriate, and its address. The name and address in Japanese are found in the outer margin of the opening page (the characters are read vertically, top to bottom), and can be shown to a taxi driver or helpful resident who may not read or speak English. Although the routes to many of the temples are marked by signs using Roman letters, at times the romanized name of the temple does not appear on its gates. By comparing the temple name printed using bold Japanese characters called *kanji*, the user of the guide should be able to match them with those on the sign. Most gardens are open from about 8:00 A.M. until 5:00 P.M.; more exact hours accompany each entry. Photography, allowed or not, is noted for each entry. Admission prices have been omitted since most range from ¥300 to ¥600.

Each entry generally consists of three parts. First, any special features are mentioned, indicating elements or characteristics of particular note in this garden. Next, the history of the garden is given, including important dates, personages, and design features. Finally, a comments section may describe noteworthy aspects of the garden's design or especially favorable times for visiting.

Maps

The novice visitor will probably experience some difficulty in getting around Kyoto, although it will be far easier to navigate in Kyoto than other Japanese cities not planned on the grid. For this reason we have included a number of maps which, although diagrammatic in nature, should provide the necessary information to get to and identify the various gardens. In *all* instances, however, the maps should be treated as diagrams, and it would be best to purchase and make reference to a more detailed Kyoto map as an adjunct.

Additional Material

At the rear of the book further listings provide sample itineraries for up to a four-day stay, an index of gardens by special features ("borrowed scenery," dry gardens, cherry blossoms, fall color), a glossary of terms, and suggested readings.

Photographs

We wish to point out that the photographs used in this book are included not only to duplicate views that can be seen by the visitor—offering a sort of preview of what will be seen—but also to serve analytical purposes. Thus, many of the photographs are taken from positions that were not intended as viewing points by the maker of the garden. A high angle or aerial photograph of the rock garden at Ryoan-ji, for example, obviously does not match what is seen from a seated position on the veranda. But this view may still be instructive for depicting the disposition of the rock clusters, the proportions of the garden, and the surrounding wall. Thus the two functions of photographs, didactic and discursive, may both be evident in certain entries.

A Note on Access and Customs

Most gardens are open to the public daily, but it should be noted that gardens will be closed at certain times of the year or on certain holidays. Some gardens are available for visits *only* for limited periods during the year; others require permission applied for in writing in advance. These restrictions will be noted, where applicable, for each garden. In general we have only included gardens accessible to the public without great difficulty. And yet an important garden such as Saiho-ji—which has closed its doors to throngs of visitors and is available only by writing—is well worth the trouble and expense if time and means permit. The Imperial Palace (Gosho) and the villas of Shugaku-in, Sento Gosho, and Katsura, are open to the public but permission must be secured in advance from the Imperial Household Agency. However, these gardens are easily available to foreigners, who are often permitted a visit on the following day, while Japanese citizens may wait months for admission. Visitors should apply at the Imperial Household Agency, near the west gate of the Gosho (Imperial Palace), allowing two to six days (depending on season). The office is open Monday–Friday 8:45–12:00 and 1:00–4:00. The office is closed Saturdays, Sundays, national holidays, and from 29 December to 3 January. Bring your passport. Most major hotels can help make these arrangements for you. The Kyoto city tourist office may also be of assistance.

The hours listed for garden access are subject to occasional change, and should be confirmed.

The visitor should note that many of the temple gardens are actually entered through buildings and often seen only from a veranda. It is the Japanese custom to remove one's shoes before entering a building. Slippers are usually provided, or visitors can walk in stocking feet. Shoes are generally left at the entry, although at some sites plastic bags are provided and the shoes are then taken along.

Orthography

Throughout the book the names of people are given in the native Japanese manner, surname first. A distinct indication of the long *o* sound, at times given as *oo*, *oh*, or *ô*, has been eliminated for the sake of simplicity. It may be helpful to note that the *-ji* or *-dera* endings of place names indicate Buddhist temples, while *-miya*, and-*jinja*, *-jingu* suffixes denote Shinto shrines.

■

Indicates inclusion in Photohistory section (Color Plates).

●

A Guide to
the Gardens
of Kyoto

The Japanese Garden and Its Cultural Context

It has little plant material; water forms neither pond nor river. Limited to rock, gravel, sand, perhaps a few pieces of moss, it embodies the reduction of the garden to its most minimal constituents. But a list of the physical elements alone does little to convey the essence of this garden, for it is not the materials in isolation that form a garden but these fragments in relationship to one another, uniting an abstract image with a realized composition. By understanding the intentions behind a dry garden such as Ryoan-ji, for example, what at first seems austere becomes incredibly rich; what at first appears meaningless becomes meaningful; what at first seems like a simple sandbox becomes—a garden.

Ryoan-ji may be the most famous and most photographed garden in the world. Only Versailles, a French garden of astronomically increased scale, can rival its celebrity. But to the untrained Western eye, Ryoan-ji's location outdoors is all that suggests that it should be considered a garden. No trees, no lawn, no flowers. No benches, paths, or ponds. This garden, in fact, may not even be entered. It exists detached like a painting or sculpture, to be viewed and considered from an appropriate distance. Ryoan-ji thus eludes our customary notion of a garden; yet to the Japanese it *is* a garden nonetheless. In gardens for the Zen sect such as these, the senses stimulate only one part of the experience; the mind provides the other part.

The dry garden, dating to the fifteenth century, was created as an aid to meditation. Its form remains timeless and classic, a supremely distilled statement of garden making. Reducing elements to define space through suggestion demonstrates the Japanese attitude toward revealing essences through implication rather than by concrete statement. This preoccupation with space and its modulation dates back further than the fifteenth century, however, to Japanese prehistory, where legends merge with physical records.

Origins and Spatial Ancestors

The precursor of the Japanese garden was the sanctified space of the Shinto shrine, a zone clearly distinguished from the natural order of its surroundings by emptying and marking. These shrines manifested ideas from both the Japanese and Chinese traditions. The fifth-century grand shrines at Ise, for example, fuse aspects of this dual heritage: the structures, almost purely Japanese in origin, derive from vernacular dwellings; the layout of the precincts draws on the monumental ordering systems of ancient China.

Two areas of concerns guide the creation of environmental form. The first attends to physical needs, protecting the body against the elements and accommodating the tasks and activities of life. The second searches for an understanding of the order and processes of nature.

The first leads to the creation of ordinary dwellings; the second to formal or monumental architecture and sacred places. Early houses in Japan were structural frames erected over an excavated pit, more a thatched roof to be occupied than a true house structure. Their form addressed the climate and topography, and revealed the limits of available technology. Settlement plans during this first phase of building, in which architecture reacted primarily to environmental conditions, evinces no sense of purposeful planning. Through the Jomon (4500 B.C.E.–200 B.C.E.) and Yayoi (200 B.C.E.–C.E. 200) eras— and even today in folk villages where flat land is scarce or the climate harsh—this apparent disorder pervades the constructed landscape. Of course, an order does govern the siting of houses and the village layout, but it is an order directed by the climate and terrain rather than by any visually conceived schema.

The change to planning with a visually perceptible order may have been an abrupt one. The years of this change have been lost to history, but by the sixth century an obvious geometric order appeared in the construction of the grand Shinto shrines at Ise. Many aspects of this geometric and clearly imported Chinese order—still represented by the primarily fourteenth-century Forbidden City in Beijing—structured the layout of spaces at Ise.

The two shrine complexes—the Naiku or Inner Shrine, and the younger Geku or Outer Shrine—clearly departed from the natural spacing and order of the great cryptomeria forest. As in the monumental Chinese city plans, these compounds were roughly symmetrical and concentric, hierarchical, and aligned on a north-south axis with the most sacred point positioned in the precinct's conceptual center. Each concentric zone was rectangular, each bounded by a series of fences. The Shoden, as the most sacred structure, not only occupied the central position in the layout, but also possessed the tallest roof. The most significant structure was thus clearly distinguished by both position and elevation.

Ise thus integrated contributions from both Chinese and Japanese sacred and palatial building traditions. The geometric order of the spaces probably entered Japan from China, but both the *torii*, or gateway, and the shrine's architectural form, derived from the raised wooden storehouse of the Yayoi period, are purely Japanese. Over time, the borrowed Chinese order was fully integrated into the Japanese spatial tradition with appropriate adaptation. But its early use, possibly as early as the third century, could imply an attempt at monumental architecture using imported ideas when native concepts did not yet match the aspirations of the builders.

In contrast to the West, Japanese architecture has prized fluid space over finite mass. The origins of this

preference may lie in Shinto, an indigenous mixture of religious beliefs whose practice centers on the worship of *kami*, or deities, and sanctifying place rather than religious image.

Kami are of two basic types: the ancestors of living Japanese, and those who pervade specific places. Unusual topographic features, such as the cave at Udo, the "wedded" twin rocks at Futami, Mt. Fuji's pure conical shape, or the mountains and rivers at Ise, all manifest the presence of kami. Appearances such as these signal sanctity and require their distinction from mundane human habitation.

In contrast to the physically enclosed walled city or cloister of the West, Japanese sacred spaces were usually suggested or implied. When spaces *were* walled, Chinese influences rather than kami were usually responsible. In Japan, gates (*torii*), fences, straw ropes (*shimenawa*), and even cloth banners demarcated spaces. Thus, shrines could constitute a mental construct more than a tangible structure, a place whose presence and limits existed more in the mind than before the eyes. Like the rock garden at Ryoan-ji, these spaces were sensed rather than viewed, although wooden structures supported the performance of ritual.

As the garden is a setting for human activity, the Shinto shrine is a setting for the kami—but the shrine is also the place where humans and deities meet. One need not travel to a heaven to meet the kami, as in Buddhism or Western religions; the kami is here, in this place, now, and always. Thus, the concern is place, not the manifestation or image of the spirit. Still, sacred spaces require identification and marking.

For every shrine at Ise there is an alternate site. For almost fifteen hundred years, with few lapses, each of the shrines has been rebuilt every twenty years in nearly the same form as a symbol of renewal. The alternate sites adjacent to the two shrines serve as formal courts, each distinguished by a surface of small stones. The positive forms of the buildings play against the void of these unplanted areas, and the white fields of stones help to denote the sacred precincts. This empty plane of gravel survived over the centuries as an element of garden planning and gradually transformed into the *yuniwa*, or formal entry court, seen in monumental architectural complexes such as the Kyoto Imperial Palace, first built in the eighth century.

Architectural historian Itoh Teiji writes in his book *The Japanese Garden:*

This yuniwa, *literally, a purified space of ground, may have been one of those broad yards covered with white gravel such as may still be seen in the Shishinden or the Seiryoden of the Imperial Palace in Kyoto. These empty yards, containing at the most a symbolic pair of trees, are like those completely graveled courts in the confines of the Ise and other ancient shrines. Such graveled courts, exorcised and hence sacred, were used to hold official and religious ceremonies and festivals.*

In time, the separation of religious and political institutions caused a divergence in the path that architecture and gardens would take. As a result, shrines retained the sacred yuniwa areas, while trees, rocks, ponds, and other elements suggesting a landscape, came to embellish these unadorned gravel areas in the palaces of the emperor and aristocracy.

Over time the nobility became more worldly and began to re-create domestic and foreign landscape scenes at their residences, some with mythic, some with specific geographic references. Elaborately planted gardens now differed markedly from the pure austerity of sacred spaces, developing into outdoor settings for pleasurable activity that might also allude to places distant or near.

As the cyclical rebuilding of Ise clearly illustrates, the early Japanese were deeply concerned with the concept of renewal. Until the founding of Nara, which from 710 to 784 served as the capital of a roughly cohered polity, the site of the capital was moved with the investiture of each new emperor. The emperor, the supreme being on earth and the nation's link with the divinity of the Sun Goddess, commanded a new locus free of all previous associations, paramount among them the death of the previous emperor. No doubt the Shinto notion of religious purification also influenced the continued remaking of the capital.

Nara Period

Until relatively recently, little has been known about the gardens of the Nara period (645–784), the era that linked the shrines at Ise with the founding of Kyoto. However, archeological findings and the layout of existing Buddhist temple complexes such as Horyu-ji have provided some clues to the planning of the gardens and their respective building groups. The description of magnificent Chinese palaces by the early Japanese embassies to the mainland contributed to formulating a palatial prototype. While the picture is not complete, it is certain that the institution of Buddhism also exerted tremendous influence on the development of religious and monumental secular architecture during this period.

Buddhism, based on the teachings of Sakyamuni, originated in India and found its way to Japan via China and Korea. Among its principal tenets was the belief in an ultimate enlightenment: insight into the true nature of all things. First introduced into Japan in 552, the year 594 marked Buddhism's official acceptance by the regent, Prince Shotoku. An avid disciple, Shotoku even today is considered one of the pivotal figures in Japanese history, not only in regards to the propagation of Buddhism, but also in terms of Japanese legal practice. Buddhism augmented rather than replaced Shinto—an accord that exists to this day.

From the sixth century on Buddhism played two key roles in the development of Japanese aesthetics. First, the religion provided a worldview and a philosophical basis for the arts and architecture; and second, it offered prototypes for the new art forms required by ritual. Images of

the Buddha fashioned by foreign craftsmen as well as copies of the sutras and religious texts entered Japan, bringing with them an iconography that had been noticeably absent in Shinto art and building. For the new temples and figurative imagery, again the Japanese initially relied on Chinese and Korean models and architectural layouts, at times emulating them without significant modification. Planning for Buddhist compounds followed the formal principles of ordering found in mainland temples and city plans, but in time builders assimilated these imported artifacts and ideas and made them an integral part of Japanese culture.

The gardens of the Nara period were also heavily influenced by Chinese prototypes, and foreign craftsmen often worked on their construction. Although no original gardens from this period remain intact, paintings of the time proffer graphic evidence of their design, illustrating naturalistic landscapes that featured bodies of water with islands and rock groupings. Period writings such as the *Manyoshu*—a collection of poetry assembled under imperial order—also contribute abundant descriptive references to gardens.

In addition, recent excavations in Nara have uncovered examples of the *yarimizu*, or river-style, garden, some of which are remarkably well preserved. This garden style, like its

Chinese Tang prototype, featured a meandering riverway punctuated by extensive rock outcroppings that collected at the end of its course as a pond. By this time, the garden had come to serve almost entirely secular programs. The nobility, who fashioned their gardens with the help of artisans and gardeners, created environments for refined pleasures, such as floating poetry composed on the spot in miniature boats down the twisting watercourses. Often extensive in size, these gardens demonstrated that the art of Japanese garden making had already achieved admirable sophistication.

Heian Period

In the succeeding centuries the art of garden building elaborated on its Nara period precedents. In palatial gardens, the pond, at first a minor feature, became its dominant element. To the immediate sensual experience was added a poetic appreciation of the seasons reflected in the garden's plants and the added dimension of literary allusion to places and people far away in time and space.

During the Heian Period (785–1184) the influence of the court first increased considerably, bringing with it a centralization of political power. By the end of the Nara period most of the main island of Honshu had fallen under the control of the Yamato court. Some clans managed to maintain some degree of independence, but the indigenous Ainu remained entrenched only in the northern portion of the island and in Hokkaido. With the ascent of Emperor Kammu in 784, the site of the capital moved first to Nagaoka for ten years and then northwest to Heian-kyo, now called Kyoto. Here the capital would remain until 1867. Kyoto became the ceremonial and cultural capital of Japan for almost a thousand years—although de facto governmental power often lay elsewhere.

The plan of Kyoto, based on the Chinese Tang capital of Changan, sited the Imperial Palace at the center of the symmetrical city: its prime position. Excepting only the pagodas of the few temples allowed within the urban boundaries, the palace was also the city's tallest structure, following precepts similar to those used in making the shrines at Ise. A circumferential drainage ditch and rampart bordered the site, also an interpretation of a Chinese model. But these earthen walls soon fell into disrepair because of their impermanent materials and overambitious length, and they were only partially reconstructed in later centuries. Graphic and literary records suggest that the original structures of the palace employed a prototypical form of the *shinden-zukuri*, a planning style that assigned different functions to individual pavilions with the Shinden, the complex's central structure, as its focus. Covered walkways connected these pavilions, which, like the buildings they joined, were elevated several feet above the ground.

On occasion the terminal pavilions extended into the garden proper, providing a covered space for landscape viewing and other worldly pleasures. (The buildings of the Gosho seen today date from 1855, the time of the last major reconstruction, and differ in style and layout from the Heian originals.)

The planning of the original palace was probably symmetrical, with two flanking pavilions used to extend the breadth of the central block and to balance its large central mass. A post-and-beam wood structure painted a brilliant vermilion-orange articulated panels of white plaster. The roofs were massive in aspect. To the south was a formal gravel court, the *yuniwa*—a broad expanse of gleaming white gravel punctuated by two solitary trees: a cherry and an orange, representing the government ministries of the left and the right. Insufficient land within the original compound precluded constructing a pleasure ground of suitable dimension, and as a result, the imperial garden of Shinsen-en lay just outside the palace proper, constructed in a suitably splendid style. Today, only a small pond and shrine occupy the site.

A limited picture of the palace and its landscape is provided by the present Heian Jingu. Although this shrine was built in 1895 at a much reduced scale, it attempted to depict the character, if not an actual representation, of Heian architecture. To the rear, or north, is a garden that incorporates stylistic features many historians believe were typical of the Heian garden, although they also convey the tastes of the times and the style of its maker, Ogawa Jihei.

The Heian garden embodied a pleasure ground that portrayed on earth a heavenly paradise. The pond was its center; around and upon it were played out many of the delights of court life. *Genji Monogatari* (The Tale of Genji) by Lady Murasaki Shikibu, written between 1001 and 1020, included extended descriptions of the lush palatial gardens where members of the imperial court amused themselves in the presence of nature. Genji, the Shining Prince, is a handsome, sensitive, and nearly irresistible protagonist whose amorous adventures and philosophical musings form the nucleus of the story. The book is also filled with passages that conjure the milieu of the time.

Murasaki's spring garden seemed only to become every day more enchanting. The little wood on the hill beyond the lake, the bridge that joined the two islands, the mossy banks that seemed to grow greener not every day but every hour—could anything have been more tempting? "If only one could get there," sighed the young people of the household and at last Genji decided that there must be boats on the lake. They were built in the Chinese style.

Akikonomu's garden was full of such trees as in autumn turn to the deepest hue. The stream above the waterfall was cleared out and deepened to a considerable distance; and that the noise of the cascade might carry further, he set great boulders in mid-stream, against which the current crashed and broke. It so happened that the season being far advanced, it was this part of the garden that was now seen at its best; here indeed was such beauty as far eclipsed the autumn splendor even of the forests near Oi, so famous for their autumn outings.

The Heian period, at least for the imperial court, was a time devoted to diverse aesthetic pursuits. During the tenth and eleventh centuries political turbulence was minimal, and much of the business of governing passed to the bureaucratic ministries. For the nobility, abundant time allowed the contemplation of the passage of seasons, boating upon the pond in Chinese-style craft, composing poetry, and sipping beverages while clad in elaborate robes of many layers.

Aristocratic life, in short, emulated an image of the heavenly sphere or, at the very least, the Japanese image of court life in China. From almost the beginning, the Japanese use of artifacts commented on its prototype rather than aiming at a faithful and absolute reproduction. Architecture and gardens evolved in

accord with Japanese values and tastes, providing settings in which to explore aesthetic interests and experience the presence of nature.

The garden played an integral part in aristocratic aesthetic life, and over time it, too, assumed a more native tone. Its rocks, ponds, and greenery served two sets of purposes: those functional and those symbolic. Functionally, a rock might reinforce an earthen bank or visually exaggerate the limits of a space or dissolve or extend a shoreline. A plant might offer a beautiful flower at a certain time of year, or a particular tree might provide cooling shade during the hot summer months. A pond could support boating or unmask delicate insects on its surface or refract colorful carp below. Like the painter who composed from a palette of impressions and features, the garden maker—whether craftsman or aristocrat—drew on the available plant and rock materials to create a scene drawn from his or her imagination.

But the garden also possessed symbolic qualities that rendered the near far away, and the seasonal, eternal. Plant groupings, rock arrangements, and islands referred to a classical, often Chinese, literary past. An island in the shape of a tortoise or crane symbolized long life, and at the same time alluded to the legendary isles of the Chinese immortals. An arrangement of rocks and trees conjured poetic references to famous sites in Japan, such as Matsushima on the northeastern coast or Ama-no-hashidate in the west. To the informed observer steeped in literature and philosophy, a small space and its natural elements opened like a series of portals to places real or mythical, distant or proximate.

The estates of the Heian period, often of considerable dimension, were usually planned by the nobles themselves in collaboration with carpenters and artisans. One of the artistic activities of the period was the creation of tray landscapes, or *bonseki,* using rocks and miniature plant materials grown for that specific purpose. With these limited means, one could create a minute garden universe—with tiny pines, stones, and a mirror for a pond. Astute planning at this scale led to an appreciation of the actual garden far beyond a casual level of inquiry. In planning the gardens, pavilions approached the shore of the pond more closely than their Chinese counterparts; in some instances, buildings on posts sat above the water. A stream usually ran along the eastern side of the grounds, feeding the pond, which emptied to the southwest—thereby satisfying the laws of the cosmos elaborated in the principles of geomancy.

Because contact with China was greatly reduced in the Heian period, the continental models altered over time, the local influences transformed arts with foreign origins: the Japa-nese style of *Yamato-e* painting, for example, evolved coevally with the Chinese-style *Kara-e.* In gardens, too, styles and concepts were digested and modified. The Japanese joined buildings and garden to merge indoor and outdoor spaces more effectively. In addition, complex curves vivified rivulets and streams, distinguishing them significantly from their continental predecessors. Ideal garden scenes followed domestic scenes to an increasing degree, and departed in significant ways from mainland landscape forms.

With further development, the river-style garden of the Nara period metamorphosed into a garden genre that recalled no specific place, but rather a generic or idealized conception. The meandering streams (*yarimizu, nosuji*) assumed the demeanor of real country streams. Natural-looking rock arrangements, local plants, and even animals furthered the quest to imitate nature. Gardens of grand scale and pictorial effects emerged as designers attempted to compose a natural setting using completely artificial means.

During the eleventh century a compilation of garden principles and planning techniques appeared as a book called the *Sakuteiki,* an amalgam of Taoist, Buddhist, and Shinto ideas that influenced design practice at this time. The *Sakuteiki* is the earliest known written document on gardening in Japan and yields insight into the nature, intentions, and sources of the aristocratic pleasure gardens.

The "large river style" (of stone arrangement) should have an appearance resembling the track left by a crawling dragon or serpent. Running water will damage what stands in its way, and banks and elevations would not keep their form without stones. Water that has struck stones veers off sharply or slowly, and is dashed (against the other side), and stones are thus necessary in some places. (As the water flows downhill it slowly modifies the character of the stream), so it is better to put stones in a manner so that the feeling gradually changes. When the banks on either side are close, the water runs rapidly, so white sand should be placed where it (the stream) is comparatively wide and the water flows gently.

By the ninth century, intrigues and political shifts had brought the Fujiwara family to political power: emperors ascended to the throne while still minors were coerced into abdicating before reaching their majority. Actual rule of the country remained in the hands of the Fujiwara regents. From this time, until the restoration of imperial rule in 1868, real political power lay in hands other than those of the emperor and the court.

South of Kyoto, at Uji, Fujiwara Michinaga erected a suburban villa

complex that included a Buddhist chapel dedicated to Amidha. His eldest son, Yorimichi, inherited the estate and constructed an even more lavish villa, although almost all of its structures have disappeared. what is left of the structures—the Byodo-in—magnificently displays the characteristics of the Heian style and stands as the prime surviving example of the era's architecture. The Phoenix Hall of the Byodo-in is symmetrically disposed, with the central hall flanked by pavilions that terminate the two horizontal extensions. Intricate beam bracketing adds to the complexity of the architectural treatment.

The woodwork of the temple has now faded to almost a natural wood graced by a delicate patina.

Originally it wore a coat of brilliant orange that contrasted strongly with the infill panels of creamy-white plaster. The building appears to be two stories high although it is, in fact, only one. The illusion is created by the mock balcony that subdivides the building's height on the exterior, a practice commonly found in the "two-story" gates of temples such as Horyu-ji.

Byodo-in is the oldest surviving example of a tradition of buildings and paradise gardens dedicated to Amidha, which includes both Kinkaku-ji, the Golden Pavilion, and Ginkaku-ji, the Silver Pavilion. Jodo Buddhism—to which the structure now serves—assured that speaking the name of Amidha would guarantee salvation and passage to the Pure Land of heaven, the Western Paradise. Amidha is characterized as the Buddha who, with his associated Boddhisattvas, presides over this celestial garden and aids in the enlightenment of all sentient beings.

A pond, said to be a re-creation of Buddha's lotus pond, reflects the Phoenix Hall and doubles its nobility and elegance. Once directly connected to the Uji River, the pond, like the building, now displays only a fraction of its former grandeur. A graceful wisteria pergola (*fuji-dana*) stands nearby on the shore, adding a touch of beauty and delicacy befitting the elegant period in which the evocative complex came into being.

Buddhism and the Samurai: The Kamakura Period

The Kamakura period (1185–1392) has left us with little physical evidence of the development of garden making. In many ways, this era exerted an impact on environmental design primarily through its philosophical contributions, that is, the ideas behind forms that reached fruition in later years. Two ethics dominated the Kamakura period: the cult of the samurai, and the related rise of Zen Buddhism as a guiding doctrine for monk and warrior.

All the Buddhist sects introduced to Japan over the centuries have affected the form of the Japanese environment, but none has had a greater influence on both the mind and the architecture of Japan than Zen. By the twelfth century, the Chinese Chan sect of Buddhism, or Zen as it came to be called by the Japanese, had been introduced by the monk Eisai and others as part of Tendai teaching. Acceptance of the new doctrine spread rapidly, and by the fourteenth century the sect was firmly entrenched, particularly within the military class (*samurai*).

Zen decisively turned from the courtly tone and intricate ritual of earlier sects. Its doctrine advocated participation in everyday life, austerity, and simplicity—as well as extended periods of meditation—to gain enlightenment and insight into the true essence of life. Enlightenment, whether or not following

13

upon years of study and meditation, was always sudden.

With the aesthetic principles that derived from it, Zen exerted a profound effect on the subsequent course of Japanese arts; virtually nothing of aesthetic consequence in any field escaped its imprint. Gardens also yielded to the values of Zen in a fundamental way, transforming them from places to delight the physical senses to places *only* to be viewed and utilized as vehicles for something greater. Zen proposed the garden as an aid to meditation—an environment to look upon, and then within. And within the small garden bounded by a simple earthen

wall arose an entire universe without bounds. At first the garden could be apprehended from a series of positions along the temple's veranda. In time, the observation point became more tightly controlled: the view opened correspondingly.

The garden at Tenryu-ji, founded in 1270 at the foot of Arashiyama in western Kyoto, was one of the first sites to reflect the changes propelled by Zen. Here the rear garden nestles at the foot of the hill and encompasses a large pond in the Heian court style. The rockwork in the pond and at its edges is particularly notable, and the visual thrust of the arrangements is decidedly vertical. This upright orientation clearly identifies the maker as sympathetic to the Chinese style—particularly the aesthetics of the Southern Song dynasty (1127–1279)—rather than to the indigenous preference for horizontality, deriving perhaps from Shinto.

Geometric order and Buddhism have already been mentioned as cultural borrowings from China; the vertical disposition of the rock clusters is another quite specific influence. But of greater importance, perhaps, was the Chinese *attitude* toward landscape and how it affected the course of Japanese landscape design.

The Chinese artist did not record geography as such but was more concerned with the phenomenal aspects of nature. Characteristics of a particular place could be treated

14   Tenryu-ji

with reverence—particularly as a means for poetic evocation—but little attempt was made to record the landscape as it was seen. Instead, artists portrayed idealized landscapes that combined feelings and impressions; in sum, an essence rather than an exact physical description. An anonymous poet of the eighth century wrote:

I would not paint a face, a rock, nor brooks, nor trees. Mere semblances of things, but something more than these. That art is best to which the soul's range gives no bound. Something besides the form, something beyond the sound.

In some respects, the gardens of the period assumed the guise of a realized painting, as both garden design and painting shared a common aspiration to a phenomenal, in some ways idealized, landscape. The two arts shared many aspects: the vertical treatment of rockwork, for example, has been mentioned, and the selective vocabulary and thoughtful juxtaposition of the made and the natural informed both the two-dimensional and three-dimensional arts. In most instances, however, the Japanese chose a more restrained composition and reduced selection of material than their mainland counterparts.

In contrast to the somewhat restless compositions of painted landscapes, the rock groupings at Tenryu-ji were calmly composed to heighten the sense of scale and space. The shoreline was muted and its contour convoluted to visually extend its perceived length. From the fourteenth century on, the number of materials would be continually pared down, culminating in gardens primarily of rock and gravel like Ryoan-ji.

Another garden of this period, Saiho-ji, popularly known as Kokedera, the Moss Temple, superbly illustrates the coevolution of religious and garden-making ideals. Unlike the secular pleasure gardens for the Heian nobility, here was a landscape of limited materials fashioned to aid religious practice. Both Saiho-ji and Tenryu-ji are associated with the Zen priest Muso Kokushi (also known as Muso Soseki, 1275–1351), who created the garden to support meditation, describing the garden in his prolific writings as a vehicle for attaining Buddhahood.

Saiho-ji represents the particular imprint of Jodo Buddhism, founded in 1175 by Honen. This garden, like the Byodo-in, is termed a "Western Paradise Garden," intended to represent the Buddha's paradise, here on earth. The subtle composition of the landscape employs little more than the soft or fluorescent greens of the mosses, the forms of tree trunks stained dark with wetness or age, and a reflecting pond: a beautiful, serene world of Buddhist imagery and religious discipline.

The Japanese social structure developed from concepts of rank and loyalties with parallels to those of Chinese Confucism. Society tended toward division into clearly defined classes: nobility and, in time, warriors at the top; then farmers, artisans, and merchants. The position and privileges of each were firmly established and precisely delineated and became further formalized by laws enacted in the seventeenth century. Limited mobility existed within these class lines, and sometimes even across them; as in many other cultures, the military presented the easiest route for advancement.

The Kamakura period, which witnessed the rise of the Minamoto and later the Hojo clans, was accompanied by the rise of the *samurai*, or warrior, class itself, with the shogun at the summit of temporal power. The samurai was a man of discipline and training, of principle and ability. He developed both his mind and body because both were seen as parts of the same entity. Governed by ethical codes, he looked at life with conviction and a sense of duty to his lord that overrode any concern for his own life.

Zen Buddhism neatly provided the samurai with a philosophical framework for training and action: it called for physical and metaphysical control, meditation, and subjugation to center the mind and establish inner calm. Zen taught austerity: simple desires, simple means. Opulence mattered little. The impotence

of the imperial court in Kyoto clearly represented the weakness bred by extravagance and lavish living. For defensive purposes, and to avoid the snares of the capital and its pleasures, the Minamoto withdrew to Kamakura near Tokyo, where they maintained a regimented lifestyle necessary to retain the skills and power needed to rule the country.

As architectural clients the Minamotos built simply. In the hilly topography of Kamakura, flat land was at a premium; little space was available to execute formal temple layouts like the extensive complexes in central Kyoto. Instead, planning schemes were simple in form, stripped of ornament, and built of natural wood with thatch or tile roofing. In terms of environmental and living patterns, military Kamakura diametrically opposed imperial Kyoto.

The Return to Kyoto: The Muromachi Period

But in Japan few have retained the reins of government without challenge. Each ruling entity suffered a decline almost from its grasp of power—a decline fostered by economic problems, alliances among opposing political or military factors, and decay from within. By the end of the fourteenth century the power base had shifted once again. The Minamoto clan, the Hojos who succeeded them, and the Kamakura shogunate as an institution, were eclipsed by the house of the Ashikaga. The new rulers returned to Kyoto, to a district of the city known as Muromachi, which lent its name to that period of Japanese history from 1393 to 1568. These years were far from happy ones. Several factions pressed claims to rule, for imperial succession, for lesser positions, and for the shogunate itself. In the 1460s these differences, compounded by famine and popular revolt, precipitated the outbreak of the Onin Wars during which the city fabric of Kyoto was almost completely destroyed.

In contrast to the political turbulence, or perhaps in direct reaction against it, an aesthetic of elegance and simplicity suffused garden design, painting, and architecture. The Heian period, the golden light in the dim past, shone as the apogee of Japanese art and culture. Patronized by the shogunate, Zen achieved its most developed doctrinal form and built its most noted architectural and landscape monuments. And eyes turned back to the eleventh and twelfth centuries, developing a preoccupation with viewing aesthetic life through a somewhat biased rearview mirror.

The values of the period—an aesthetic later steeped in tea as well as Zen—produced Ryoan-ji and the dry garden. The *cha-no-yu*, or tea ceremony, evolved into a formal custom by the late sixteenth century

and increasingly influenced the design of gardens as settings for retreat from the everyday world.

Ashikaga Yoshimitsu, third of the Ashikaga shoguns, established a precedent for the period by erecting Kinkaku, the Golden Pavilion, one of the most celebrated buildings in Japanese architecture. Since its builder followed Jodo Buddhism, the building program made overt reference to earlier Western Paradise gardens such as the Byodo-in and Saiho-ji. In style, the pavilion is a sophisticated mixture of Japanese and Chinese architectural ideas, but the blending is so subtle and complete that in the final analysis the architecture must be called Japanese. Some aspects of the building's disposition and detailing recall the land across the sea, but the delicacy and elegance of its resolution, and the perfection of its proportions in small elements as well as in overall structure are, ultimately, domestic.

The Kinkaku stands half in the water, half on the shore, using the large pond to mirror the building and the surrounding hills and landscape. Skillful arrangements of rocks, islands, and trees extend the vistas from the building and exaggerate the sense of dimension across the water. All the elements of the garden's composition are so carefully contrived and finely balanced that they create the impression of an untouched natural area. If the extravagances of the Heian period were unattainable because of

17

the demands of the age, one could at least make overt poetic references to them. Thus, through allusion and illusion associations with the gardens and aesthetics of the golden age could be forged.

The pond gardens used for refined activities such as boating and writing poetry opposed the dry, or *kare-sansui*, gardens that served more as symbolic spaces for meditation and viewing. The new Muromachi garden returned viewers to the planted areas rather than confining them to the veranda. One did not observe this garden from a single point, like a stage set, but instead surveyed, traversed, smelled, listened, and appreciated its merits from many positions in space. The richly vegetal landscape, which in any period of Japanese history almost always coexisted with other more austere types, emerged as a leading garden form, reaching its culmination in the later stroll gardens of the seventeenth century.

In 1482 the eighth Ashikaga, Yoshimasa, constructed his pavilion and garden on the eastern side of Kyoto as a retreat from the exigencies of the times, again extending the tradition of the paradise garden and its association with the Amidha Buddha. In deference to his grandfather, who had built the Golden Pavilion, this building was named the Silver Pavilion, Ginkaku. Yoshimasa never intended to cover the pavilion in silver and thus the name was only metaphorical.

The garden at Ginkaku-ji continues to puzzle students of the Japanese landscape with its diverse elements set in raucous juxtaposition. Today, between the delicacy of the plant materials and the architectural frame of the temple buildings stretches a broad mound of raked sand and a tall truncated cone of sand adjacent to it. According to some philosophies, the harmony and unity of the garden are shattered by these elements—in all probability later additions and not part of the original garden—and the aesthetic experience consequently suffers. According to others (with which the authors concur), this apparent contradiction contributes immeasurably to the garden's success.

One element, one material, or one form, can define another through contrast. The antithetical expression of one system can positively express another: opposites define what they *are,* as well as what they are *not.* At Ginkaku-ji, living material plays against sand maintained in a raked, and thus obviously constructed, state.

Interpreting the sand/plant relationship in this way draws on Zen and Shinto as sources of explanation. In Zen the *koan,* or conundrum, was used as a stimulus for training or perhaps even for achieving sudden enlightenment. The philosophical stance of Zen readily admits contradiction as a part of existence—

in fact, its doctrine suggests that Zen effaces the idea of opposites, and variations in materials and order are therefore but minor deviations in the great scheme of things. Seeming contradictions inject power, presence, and strength to the expression and meaning in the garden. Rather than detracting from the whole, new and unusual order and experience result.

The Reductivist Aesthetic: The Dry Garden

Despite their impressive beauty, the gardens of the Golden and Silver Pavilions represent only one type of Muromachi garden. In contrast to the copiously planted materials of these estates, which continued the paradise garden tradition, was the simplicity of the dry Zen garden. Zen increased its appeal in an era of external unrest by offering internal spiritual peace without unnecessarily elaborate doctrine and ritual. In times of civil turmoil the temple often served as an actual as well as spiritual refuge. Major religious compounds such as Daitoku-ji and

Ginkaku-ji

spiritual refuge. Major religious compounds such as Daitoku-ji and Myoshin-ji extended their size and influence by grouping numerous sub-temples under the jurisdiction of a single abbot. The walled enclosures of the sub-temples, each fitted and adjusted to an existing context, play against the formal alignment of the main gate, lecture hall, and main hall. The continued addition of new structures and gardens effectively precluded the extension of the monumental building core in any formal manner, resulting in the less regular disposition of domestic architectural forms that characterized the residential zones.

Many gardens today considered the finest representatives of the Zen aesthetic were the products of the fifteenth and sixteenth centuries. Although space available for making gardens was limited, illusionary space was ever abundant. Few garden forms can rival the austere dry garden for its sense of a universe within four walls. Ryoan-ji and Daisen-in are the foremost representatives of this type with their precisely raked gravel and dynamic groupings of stones. The landscape forms look inward, neatly paralleling the religious introspection and tranquility found within the precincts and their religious practices.

At Daisen-in, a sub-temple of Daitoku-ji dating from 1509, a narrow passage opens to a garden barely twelve feet in depth. Like a simplified, yet three-dimensional realization of a painted landscape, the garden was painstakingly constructed, using an imaginative placement of stones and a punctured screen wall to invoke a sense of deep space. Only slightly larger in dimension is the cluster of rocks that forms the primary scene. Intended to be viewed frontally, this invocation of a mountain landscape creates an illusion of surprising depth through a complex and masterful composition of stones and sparse plant material.

The skilled use of the simplest means, in areas of restricted measure, created a quiet world of beauty within the temple walls. The scenes were reduced in medium but highly symbolic; frugality was the prevailing virtue. Elements of the natural landscape, abstracted within a miniature palette, produced gardens that embodied Zen belief, finding endless fascination in spaces ascetic in their stricture.

A number of these gardens portend twentieth-century abstract painting in their use of essential elements to suggest greater forms and landscapes. Other gardens replicated in three dimensions the then-popular concepts of landscape paintings. But in all its varied forms the dry garden defied physical, if not philosophical, convention. Whether restricted to rock and sand, or allowed to luxuriate in more elaborate plantings, the gardens of the Muromachi period exhibited some of the most strikingly original garden forms of all time.

Refined Poverty

Accompanying the increased popularity of ritualized tea drinking, the so-called tea ceremony, came a garden setting to enhance the experience. At first only a room of a villa or temple was devoted to the ceremony; in time that room became a simple detached house, poetically regarded as a "rustic hut in the woods." The tea garden or *roji* ("dewy path"), differed from other gardens in that it led to the tea ritual: it was a vehicle for transition more than an elaborate landscape in and of itself. Movement and transition, both physical and psychological, underwrote its design.

Tea had been imported from China perhaps as early as the fifth century, but the practice of Zen benefited from a stimulant to maintain wakefulness and concentration during extended periods of seated meditation, and this accelerated its adoption. With this new use and broader availability, the consumption of tea became more widespread, although still primarily dedicated to stimulant or medicinal purposes.

In time, the aristocracy adopted the beverage for less than functional situations. Tea parties introduced different species of teas from many locations and tested the palates and sophistication of their guests. Over time, tea tasting became more and more ritualized, resulting in another transformation of meaning. And by the sixteenth century, a more definite outline for the tea ceremony had been confirmed.

Still, at this time the ritual and its implements were regarded as malleable and capable of greater perfection. Later tea masters, particularly those active at the close of the sixteenth century, modified the ritual, augmenting and discarding, forming, developing, and reforming to suit their individual tastes. Armed with the concept of *mitate*, tea masters continued their invention, accepting nothing—whether implement or practice—as given or final. Freely translated as "re-seeing," or "borrowed metaphor," mitate provided a way of viewing in a new light, or elevating the most mundane to the highest aesthetic plane.

The great tea masters, especially Sen no Rikyu, Kobori Enshu (who reshaped the Japanese garden), and Furuta Oribe, established the antecedents that directed the ceremony's further elaboration. In the mind of a genius like Rikyu, tea reached a philosophical perfection that became nearly impossible to surpass, although it is still constantly developing— at least in theory.

Tea implied simplicity, and simplicity in turn implied the culture of the everyday—particularly the *rural* everyday. Early tea masters believed that the folk cultures of rural Japan lived in the closest harmony with the land. For unlike the products of the less restricted palette of materials, colors, forms, foreign influences, and construction techniques found in the major cities, those of folk culture remained unspoiled, simple, and truthful. Rural life was thus a model of moral excellence and therefore represented the highest order of beauty and perfection. Its acceptance of imperfection—an acceptance perhaps grounded in pragmatism—was seen as its very perfection.

The "hut in the woods" that offered a poetic prototype for the teahouse was usually quite small—only four-and-a-half *tatami* mats in area. Although its architectural model was the aristocratic architecture of

the temple or villa, "refined poverty" was the desired feeling. Painted surfaces and gilded screens were eschewed; the tea room abhorred decoration, opting instead for asymmetry executed in natural materials: tatami, mud plaster, exposed wood.

The focus of the room was the *tokonoma,* or ceremonial alcove, that contained the single hanging scroll or flower arrangement. This solitary display, with the implements of the ceremony—the kettle, tea bowl, tea caddy, tea whisk, and tea scoop— were the only possible deviations from the basic neutrality of the interior. The entire ensemble was conceived as an environment of equilibrium and repose for transcending the cares of daily life.

The roji carried guests from the everyday world to that of tea. The garden presented a gradation of order from more formal arrangements of planting at the entrance to seemingly informal and less structured aspects near the tea house. The experience of the garden depended heavily on the placement of the stepping stones that comprised the path. By using irregular intervals and surfaces, the designer could choreograph movement and view, coaxing guests to look down while watching each step, to exaggerate the effect, or reveal a new vista or nuance of the garden's design. Control of movement became control of feeling and effect.

The arrangement of rough and finished stones in the path borrowed the calligraphic principle of *shin-gyo-so*—formal, semiformal, and informal—that was fundamental to all Japanese environmental design in this and later periods. Mixtures of formalities within the sequence enriched the overall transition from more structured areas to those more informal. The path of irregular rounded stones might intersect or reinforce a stone plank, or "bridge"; formal elements almost always confronted more informal stones. On occasion a discarded millstone, for example, was "re-seen" and integrated into the composition as another application of mitate—its appeal based doubly on its acquired history and geometric form.

Stories about the tea masters are legendary and often concern Sen no Rikyu specifically. Two vignettes provide an insight into the nature of the masters.

Rikyu, it is said, had grown a beautiful expanse of morning glories as part of his tea garden—rare flowers of an exceptional beauty. His arrogant patron and antagonist Toyotomi Hideyoshi, then the ruler, extorted an invitation to tea to view these flowers about which he had heard so much. At first Rikyu demurred, but under continued pressure he deferred to his superior.

Arriving at the garden, Hideyoshi viewed the familiar scene with no hint of the prized blooms, for they had been removed. Losing his calm—bad manners when invited to tea—he entered the teahouse in a rage. But once inside he quickly regained his composure: there, as the prized element of a flower arrangement in the tokonoma—was a single morning glory, the queen of the entire collection.

The second story concerns garden design more directly. It is said that one garden poised high on the side of the hill possessed a spectacular vista of the sea, but tall hedges completely surrounded its bounds. As guests walked through the garden the hedges denied even a glimpse of the ocean; instead, the focus fell within the garden itself.

Before entering, however, guests bent over the stone water basin to rinse their mouths as part of their symbolic purification before partaking of tea. There, through a small hole cut cleanly in the hedge just above the basin, they gloried at an intensified and moving view of the sea. Thus, not only did they rediscover the distant water, but they also forged a symbolic linkage between the water confined within the basin and the water in the vast oceans beyond.

Opulence Again

Like the tides, Ashikaga power reached its height and then ebbed, as clan power had risen and fallen time and time before. With nearly continuous military campaigns, Oda Nobunaga nearly brought Japan to true unification, rather than a state riddled by conflicting power blocs. Murdered by one of his staff, Nobunaga was succeeded by Toyotomi Hideyoshi, mentioned earlier in relation to Sen no Rikyu and tea. Hideyoshi succeeded where Nobunaga had failed, and consolidated the power of nonimperial rule to one of almost absolute control.

In this era of castle building Hideyoshi built his own castle, south of Kyoto, in the Fushimi Momoyama district. As in the Muromachi period, the castle hill and its surrounding district lent their name to the era, the Momoyama period (1569–1603).

This was an age characterized by opulence and ornamentation, with a nouveau-riche aesthetic antithetical to the "refined poverty" of tea—though the simplicity of the tea aesthetic continued to flourish and develop in parallel to the newer style. The Sambo-in, whose design Hideyoshi directly influenced, best represents the gardens of this period.

The problem of overabundant materials plagued the making of the Sambo-in garden, and it is difficult to regard its composition as harmonious. To aesthetes and garden makers of the time, plant materials and rocks possessed exceptional value and, in some instances, held status as nearly priceless objects. Garden workers might commit suicide or enter exile if a prime botanical specimen or a rock under their care was damaged. Occasion-ally garden materials were commandeered from lesser lords, and prize stones and plants given to superiors as meaningful symbols of selfless devotion.

Hence, through gifts, intrigue, and subtle suggestion, Hideyoshi had accumulated a considerable aggregation of garden material for remaking the Sambo-in near his castle at Fushimi Momoyama. The gardener Kentei spent almost twenty years working and reworking the garden's form, continuing even after Hideyoshi's death. Although almost devoid of visual calm, the landscape breathes visual provocation. For the modernist taste, however, too many features compete for attention. No matter how skillfully the rocks were set and transitional materials interspersed, too many elements thwart reading the garden as congenial.

Yet the Sambo-in is significant in other ways. In spatial transitions and the earth-covered bridges— bridges that link the banks psychologically in addition to spanning them—the garden points to the fully developed stroll gardens of the succeeding Edo period. By representing the practice of inclusion this garden contradicts the simplicity of the tea garden and the austerity and symbolism of the monastic dry garden, and perhaps better represents the taste of its age.

The transition from the sixteenth to seventeenth centuries witnessed yet another shift in design attitude.

The influences of Zen, tea, and indigenous religious beliefs have been discussed. In time these three streams blended sufficiently to establish an aesthetic stance best stated in Günter Nitschke's term: "sophisticated order."

In contrast to the regularity and clear structure of geometric planning, sophisticated order stimulated the initial impression of asymmetrical disorder. No clear axes governed; nothing *seemed* planned although, in fact, everything had been meticulously conceived and executed. The human hand was so underplayed that in its final form, to the viewer the garden appeared natural. This was the goal.

But the garden never was natural. It continued to be, as it always had been, an idealized landscape. Tradition still exerted influence; the garden never followed a drastic change of course. Formal geometric elements appeared with naturalistic layouts although the relative balance of formal and informal parts had been considerably readjusted.

The gradual stylistic development is seen best in the plans of Buddhist temple compounds. Geometric order entered Japan by the sixth century, reigned through the thirteenth century, and guided the layout of major symmetrical complexes like the Kyoto Imperial Palace and the Miyajima shrine on Itsukushima. In time, however, the allure of axial symmetry faded. Evident geometry and symmetry often required expanses of flat land all too rare in Japan, and even when level terrain was available, rice growing usually took precedence over habitation.

In mountain districts such as Koyasan or on Mt. Hiei in Kyoto, the central grouping of temple structures employed axial alignment as best it could. The layout of the entire temple, however, expanded over the centuries on individual plots of land, each fitted to the last as expediently as possible. This form of contextualism, of fitting new parts to the old, marked a pattern of growth that paralleled the growth of organisms in nature.

The temple of Daitoku-ji, northwest of the Imperial Palace, exemplifies the patchwork of spaces and buildings resulting from additive growth to a symmetrically ordered core. The compound included over twenty sub-temples, each complete with its own buildings and gardens, each with a wall to separate the sub-temple from the outside world. The positioning of structures within the walls created several unroofed spaces between the buildings, including the forecourt or entry, and the side and main gardens. At Daitoku-ji, entry to the Superior's quarters was gained by passing through a simple dry garden punctuated by two symmetrical cones of sand. Architecture began not under the roof of the temple but already within the walled garden. Thus, each temple was distinct in its planning and arranged to accommodate its own particular functions and patterns of growth. The Daitoku-ji complex as an entirety, on the other hand, reflects a concern with incremental collective form as the sum total of sub-temple development.

Edo Period

Hideyoshi's death in 1598 once again raised the question of succession. Governmental power did not ultimately rest with Hideyoshi's son Hideyori, however, but instead with one of his generals, Tokugawa Ieyasu, who in earlier years had also served Nobunaga. In short order Ieyasu conclusively established his position as shogun, the de facto ruler, and laid a foundation for rule by regulation that continued until the forced opening of the country in the nineteenth century.

The major social and military problems were handled expediently. A system of fiefs, based on marital ties or length of loyalty to the Tokugawa clan, concentrated the power. Geographic positioning of trusted families, and restrictions on those whose fidelity was not firmly established, averted thoughts of outright rebellion. Sumptuary laws structured virtually every aspect of life including building and garden making, personal expenditure, and social activities. For almost three centuries, the Tokugawas ruled relatively unchallenged.

Under the Tokugawa regime Japan was closed to almost all foreign trade, and ultimately foreign knowledge; the reign was introverted and sequestered. Catholic priests, who had arrived in the late 1500s, were expelled along with other foreigners as potential threats to political stability. Japan's sole window on the world was the Dutch trading colony on Dejima in Nagasaki, maintained under the watchful eyes of Tokugawa authorities. Commodore Matthew Perry's sudden arrival in 1853 would catalyze a showdown that ultimately led to the downfall of the shogunate by exposing its internal political and military weaknesses. But until that time, Japan's image reflected back on itself in the arts, traditions, ceremonies, and environmental design, assimilating earlier foreign influences in the process.

The Flowering of the Stroll Garden

The Edo period (1603–1867) embraced aesthetic heterogeneity. Culturally, Japan has functioned as if it were a prehistoric lake into which additions from each era settle and accumulate, layer upon layer, like sedimentary rock. Some attitudes or styles are adjusted, modified, and assimilated. Others remain inert and intact—distinctly identifiable in any context.

This period's gift to Japanese landscape heritage is epitomized in the gardens of three imperial building projects: the Katsura Villa, the Sento Gosho, and the Shugaku-in Villa. Not only do these gardens superbly display potent design concepts such as planning and movement along the diagonal, "hide-and-reveal," and "borrowed scenery," but they also exploit these ideas with elegance and sophistication.

During the early Edo period, gardens at Shoden-ji, Entsu-ji, and Joju-in skillfully utilized *shakkei*, or borrowed scenery, although its most effective application appears in the upper garden at Shugaku-in. In a similar way, Katsura offers a veritable museum of hide-and-reveal planning and diagonal movement, as well as almost every other aspect of Japanese spatial design. Like Katsura, the Sento Gosho applied historical and literary allusion embodied in an eloquent vegetal setting in which experience through movement prevailed.

The early 1600s were a time of active building, as the nation settled into a relatively peaceful time controlled by Tokugawa governmental structure. The emperor, always the divine embodiment of the state, remained ensconced in Kyoto; but the shogunate now moved for the last time, to Tokyo, or Edo as it was then known.

Using the years provided by the customary early retirement, the emperor created an artistic environment for the court, his family, and himself. In creating his gardens, Emperor Gomizuno (1596–1680),

like many before him, turned his eye to the past, particularly to the paradise pond gardens of the Heian Period. His Sento Gosho southeast of the existing Imperial Palace centers on a pond; its gardens endure although fire destroyed the buildings in the nineteenth century. Like many historical gardens, however, it exists only in modified form.

The path through the Sento Gosho effectively applied the design principle of hide-and-reveal, using movement to manipulate the kimono-clad courtier using sequential focal points to heighten the sense of both space and arrival. Unlike the formal arrangements of Western planning such as the nearly contemporary Versailles, hide-and-reveal spurned the use of axes.

With straight lines and exact geometry, French formal gardens of the seventeenth century effected their axial symmetry with a vengeance. The clear axis manifested the power of the autocrat—Louis XIV—over nature and the people. Walking on axis, the visitor senses movement and progression, but the eye always fixes on the end of the axis, which remains the goal.

In contrast, hide-and-reveal fixes attention on the proximate as one stage in a continuous procession. Rather than follow a straight line, the path veers: first left to appreciate a tree, then perhaps right to glimpse a rock grouping on the pond's shore. Irregular placement of step-

landscape gardeners William Kent, Capability Brown, and Humphry Repton. The Japanese were studious observers of life. They felt that in nature each organism was always complete—in birth, growth, fruition, and even death—and they used this belief to make landscapes that did not require years of growth to appear complete.

One technique for garden making was the planning of building groups and movement along a diagonal. Unlike Western buildings, which are approached frontally, implying confrontation, Japanese buildings of this period were approached obliquely, on the diagonal. When viewed in this way the building within its garden setting was less a terminus than another carefully considered feature of the landscape. In architecture the diagonal was often suggested if seldom visible. Most buildings comprised rectilinear and modular elements based on the roughly three-by-six foot dimensions of the tatami mat. Structural stability derived from the rigid joints of the building's wooden structural frame—rather than from triangulation in the walls—and from the dead weight of the hulking roof.

ping stones coaxes guests to look down to watch their step; looking up, a new vista of the garden unfolds. They follow the shoreline marveling at the restrained palette of plant materials selected to change color and shape throughout the year. Like nature itself, the garden assumes different forms in different seasons; each year, every year. Like the modulation of views, the garden's form emerges not in one visit, but only over time.

The Japanese understood nature in a manner uncommon to the West. Nature was the model for the natural. The closest Western parallel is the English landscape garden tradition of the eighteenth and nineteenth centuries as practiced by

In the Katsura Villa the aesthetic use of the diagonal is readily apparent. The three building wings, or *shoin*, are staggered in a loose V-form, termed a "geese in flight" arrangement. The shoins could, and did, develop in three distinct stages,

as they were built over the period of
almost a century. But at each stage
the form read as complete and in
harmony with its environment.
Crossing the final bridge at Katsura,
one acquires an unobstructed view
of the villa's three pavilions: the
path approaches as neither parallel
nor perpendicular to the buildings'
surfaces, but diagonal to them.

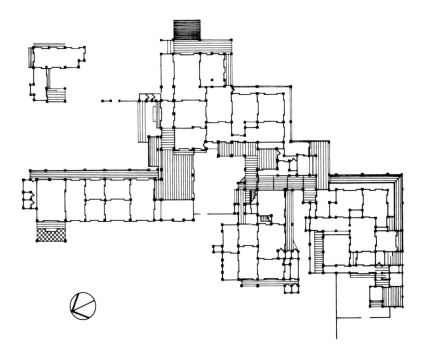

Katsura Rikyu: Plan of the Shoin

Borrowed scenery (*shakkei*) was another principle dramatically applied during the Edo period, despite its deceptively simple basis. The private garden occupies the foreground of a desired vista. Planting, hedges, or walls screen undesirable visual elements in the middle ground, such as a neighboring house or inappropriate natural features, and effect a smooth transition from the foreground to the background features. Although lying far beyond the reaches of one's own land, the background feature is appropriated and incorporated into the garden as part of the visual composition. At the temple of Entsu-ji in northern Kyoto a green hedge at the garden's edge bounds a rock arrangement in the garden's foreground. Above the hedge one grasps a majestic view of Mt. Hiei in the distance, layered into the garden space as if in a woodblock print.

Most skilled applications of shakkei are impressive, but nowhere is borrowed scenery more spectacularly employed than at the imperial villa of Shugaku-in. Emperor Gomizuno built the twenty-three acre garden as a retreat at which to withdraw for rest and undisturbed contemplation. There are three gardens at Shugaku-in—lower, middle, and upper—each skillfully devised and beautifully planted, but of these the upper garden is by far the most dramatic.

From the middle garden the imperial guests walked between the rice fields and turned abruptly uphill along the formal, gently curving avenue. The pines planted in the Meiji period today provide a feeling of closure, and their equidistant planting creates a rhythm that diminishes fatigue from the uphill walk. The large dam to the left retains the pond of the upper garden; its stepped profile reduces the apparent mass of its mammoth earthen wall and is barely distinguishable from the terraces of the rice fields. A thatched gate opens on narrow stone steps, bounded on both sides by a tall hedge that restricts the view and directs attention to the steps themselves. The turning stairs climb within these constricting green walls.

Reaching the summit, guests arrive facing a small pavilion—yet sensing a presence behind them. Turning, a vast panorama greets astonished eyes. Trees, woods, a reflecting lake, and in the distance, a superb vista of the surrounding mountains, all are drawn in as parts of the garden. Although the view would be magnificent under any conditions, it is almost overwhelming when contrasted to the confined approach that preceded it. Here the three principles—approach on the diagonal, hide-and-reveal, and borrowed scenery—interweave to craft a landscape tapestry of delicacy, grandeur, and impressive beauty.

Other Edo gardens applied key properties of effective site planning resulting in complex and unique environments. The entire complex of the temple Kiyomizu, for example, dramatically sits astride a narrow ridge as a broad platform flung against the hillside, supported by a grid of wooden columns and beams that support, in addition, an enormous roof of shingled thatch. Each of the buildings contributes to the composition of the complex as a whole: none could be repositioned without seriously detracting from the effect of the ensemble. Kiyomizu superbly exemplifies a sophisticated order that at first appears random, particularly in the relationship of the buildings on the ridge to the stream below. But this first appearance is deceptive—its order may not be apparent, but order unquestionably pervades the design.

Below the main hall at Kiyomizu, to the north, is the sub-temple of Joju-in. In this garden borrowed scenery is used in a slightly different way than at Shugaku-in. By correlating a stone lantern within the garden with a second on the opposite hill, the garden's design visually extends across the intervening ravine. Using analogous forms, this relation of the near to the far stretches the limits of the garden to enfold the surrounding hills and sky. Joju-in shows how one basic concept, borrowed scenery, can be modified and manipulated to produce an inventive work within a traditional framework.

The use of the clipped hedge produced works of considerable interest during the Edo period, with the gardener and tea devotee Kobori Enshu (1579–1647) its master. Enshu is usually referred to as Japan's first landscape architect because he was among the first to work on garden design as a professional, rather than an accomplished amateur. Numerous gardens have been credited to him (including Joju-in mentioned above), although they probably were executed or even designed by his associates.

Two gardens assigned to Enshu with some certainty are the Konchi-in at Nanzen-ji in Higashiyama, and Daichi-ji in neighboring Shiga prefecture, although the latter attribution is less sure. At Konchi-in, the dense shrubbery is shaped into several distinct clusters that counter the openness of a sheet of raked gravel. Dating from about 1632, the garden can be viewed as a transitional style, or more accurately, an amalgam of dry and planted garden traditions. Whatever its classification, the design elegantly plays animate against inanimate, and effectively modulates the movement from the veranda to the stone edging, to the gravel, to the bordering hedge.

At Daichi-ji, some sixty kilometers from Kyoto, the sheared hedge reached an apotheosis and most closely approached the topiary tradition of the West. Although the practice might be analogous, the

exudes a rhythmic undulation in itself. As an entirety the garden ultimately acquires an equilibrium, but it is hardly at rest. Although the clipped shrub appears to excellent effect in other gardens, Katsura Rikyu and Shisen-do among them, at Daichi-ji no other garden features challenge its dominance.

Through the Dutch trading colony at Nagasaki the shogunate peeped at the events and culture of the West, and a select handful of Japanese scrutinized the small but constant trickle of Western ideas that arrived at the Dejima settlement. But the country was physically and legally closed—closed to foreigners trying to land or trade there, and closed to Japanese wanting to travel abroad.

intent and effect differed considerably in Japan. At Vaux-le-Vicomte, designed by André le Nôtre in the 1660s, trees as living sculptures maintained an idealized form. Arranged in a precise and rhythmic progression, they constituted transitional elements, linking the forms of statues with those of landscape.

This isolation nurtured an introspection responsible for assimilating previously imported concepts and philosophies more completely into Japanese culture. It has been said that the history of Japan's use of foreign ideas has been "adopt, adapt, adept." This dictum applies equally to Japanese garden art. By the seventeenth century, Japan had surpassed its cultural parent China in creating landscapes of beauty and intricacy. The student had become the teacher.

At Daichi-ji, on the other hand, the hedge *is* the garden, with the ground plane as the negative space for the figure of the hedge and its auxiliary plant material. Like the dense black of *sumi* ink in Zen calligraphy, the mass of azaleas is dense and opaque, twisting and turning in space like a captive dragon or landlocked wave. Rather than only one element of a progression, the hedge

Opening the Door

The appearance of the American Commodore Matthew Perry's black ships in Tokyo Bay in 1853 decisively ended Japanese seclusion.

In the era of the Meiji (Imperial) Restoration (1868–1911), traditional culture was discarded wholesale. Most eyes turned West.

In architecture, strange concoctions of Western forms and Japanese building techniques normally used for castles and storehouses sprang up in the foreigners' residential districts of open ports like Hakodate, Yokohama, and Kobe. Railroads were built and telegraph wires extended across the land, or at least along the coasts where construction was feasible. Under government sponsorship Japan industrialized quickly, and the country matured into a major political and economic power by 1905. In a mere thirty-five years Japan moved in technological proficiency from the eighteenth to the twentieth century.

Interest in traditional gardens dwindled. A conservative element backed by the former nobility desperately tried to maintain the practice, creating gardens such as Murin-an and the Heian Jingu. But in the path of industrialization these were isolated attempts, ineffectual as a force, and in time they bowed under. Many traditional art forms were eclipsed by Western forms like sculpture and genre oil painting. Foreigners such as Edward Morse, Ernest Fenollosa, and Josiah Conder, who wrote a classic text on the Japanese garden, tried to turn the Japanese view back to the old aesthetic traditions—but with little success.

Japanese gardens require immense amounts of care, their naturalistic appearance notwithstanding, and without continued maintenance they deteriorated rapidly. The disenfranchised nobility lacked the funds to maintain large gardens, and the government had other, more pressing items on its agenda. Although interest in gardens continued in the twentieth century, it was at best the maintenance of an ossified tradition. Some additions and restorations were undertaken in the 1930s, but it was only after the Pacific War that the popularity of gardens increased at a rapid pace. Shigemori Mirei, Nakane Kinsaku, and Mori Osamu are perhaps the best known of a talented group of landscape designers who brought the Japanese garden into the twentieth century with inventive new works, or extended tradition in numerous restorations and reconstructions of venerable gardens.

The Japanese Garden in Modern Times

In the postwar era gardens gained a new status. Twentieth-century Western architecture luckily found useful parallels in traditional Japanese architecture (see Walter Gropius' introduction to Tange Kenzo's book on the Katsura Villa). The concepts of Japanese design—space-time (the experience of architecture in time), the use of modular planning, the open plan, and spatial flexibility—intrigued Western design professionals. Japanese architects and designers reexamined their heritage and again tried (often desperately) to amalgamate the two traditions.

After the war, governmental programs aimed at reconstructing heavy industry and housing; little funding remained for recreational purposes. Hence, cultural institutions like the temple gardens served new recreational and leisure uses. The imperial villas were opened to the public on a limited basis, and interest in gardens increased among the natives as well as foreign visitors. New discoveries were made on ancient sites, and the restoration of many gardens began.

The foreign tourists who visit Japan are usually less interested in bastard examples of Western culture than in lasting vestiges of traditional Japan. That is the good news. Now for the bad news. Although tourism does help maintain the gardens through admission fees and sales of publications that accrue considerable sums of money, the flow of thousands of foreign and native tourists adversely affects fragile wooden buildings, tatami floors, and the delicate plants of which gardens are made. Many gardens have restricted their hours, or have closed their gates entirely, in an effort to preserve what remains of their centuries-old environments.

Pollution also has taken its toll, and in Tokyo the major gardens have never recovered their Edo period splendor. Even if plants could prosper under these unfavorable environmental conditions, the din of traffic and machinery does little to foster a setting for contemplation—nor does the borrowed scenery of an office block or television tower contribute more to the garden's composition than a disruptive note.

But despite these assaults on gardens by modern urban life, fortunately much remains. Through the centuries Japan has forged a landscape tradition with a unique perspective and palette. The gardens may seem only "pretty" to the casual visitor, but with even rudimentary study one can recognize and peel away the layers of association and meaning that lead to a more complete appreciation of the gardens. The Japanese garden offers rich experiences that develop over time and change constantly from season to season. Carefully conceived, it is a naturalistic landscape that accepts progress and the cycles of nature as part of its design. It is a garden to be seen, felt, and considered—a living environment for both the body and mind. The gardens of Kyoto offer a superb—indeed matchless—collection of landscape art, and a unique Japanese cultural expression. Here in Kyoto, culture is written in the landscape.

Photohistory (Color Plates)

Saiho-ji, 1339. *(p 107).*

Kinkaku-ji, 1395. *(p 96).*

Ginkaku-ji, c. 1480. *(p 127).*

Taizo-in, Myoshin-ji; 15th c. *(p 86).*

Ryoan-ji, 1499. *(p 93)*.

Sambo-in, 1395. *(p 185)*.

Koto-in, Daitoku-ji; c. 1603. *(p 63).*

Nijo-jo; 1603, 1624–6. *(p 77).*

Katsura Rikyu, 1620. *(p 110).*

Joju-in, 1629. *(p 168).*

Sento Gosho, 1634. *(p 73)*.

Shisen-do, 1636. *(p 131)*.

41

Shugaku-in Rikyu, 1659. *(p 135)*.

Zuiho-in, Daitoku-ji; 1961. *(p 69)*.

Making the Landscape of Kyoto

The year 1867 witnessed crucial changes in the political and cultural institutions of Japan. The preceding fourteen years, since Perry's appearance in Tokyo Bay, had brought upheaval in almost all areas of life. But with the restoration of power to the imperial agency, and the coronation of Emperor Meiji, a new era was beginning. Japan, after centuries of seclusion, was turning its interests toward modernization and participation in a world community. The capital was officially transferred to Edo and renamed Tokyo—Eastern Capital. After a thousand years as the imperial capital, Kyoto now relinquished its title. But Kyoto, imperial city, retained its heritage as the central repository of Japanese material culture, and its architecture and gardens testified to its claim. In time, Tokyo would house the Diet and the economic forces behind the country's production—but Tokyo could not begin to rival the wealth of buildings, temples, villas, and palaces, indeed the very sense of history that Kyoto possessed.

To understand the culturally commanding position that Kyoto occupies, it is useful to examine the traditions of city building that preceded its creation. Kyoto had not always been the capital of Japan. Until the seventh century, the residence of the emperor, that is, the de facto capital, changed with each successive reign. The *Kojiki*, one of the two first historical chronicles—a mixture of myth and history compiled in 711—lists the succession of imperial rule and its peripatetic residences. During the Kofun period (roughly the fourth through mid-sixth centuries), great burial mounds marked the resting place of each emperor. Immense in bulk and impressive in dimension, these tombs came to dot the Yamato Plain around Nara, bearing witness to the growing influence and nomadic habits of the ruling clan, as well as to the demand for a new capital that accompanied ritual purification after an imperial death.

But by the eighth century such movement had more or less ceased. Perhaps the increasing population and its domestic burdens had rendered continued resettlement too costly and time consuming. Perhaps the increasing influence of Buddhism weakened the Shinto belief requiring purification and renewal after death. In Heijo-kyo, now known as Nara, a new capital was established during the reign of Empress Gemmei in 708, and occupied in 710. It was to remain the capital for seventy-four years, until the reign of Emperor Kammu.

At this time, Japan was politically little more than the single Yamato district, which was gradually strengthening its hold on the diverse settlements of the country. There were as yet only small fragments of an urban tradition. In building the new capital city, the

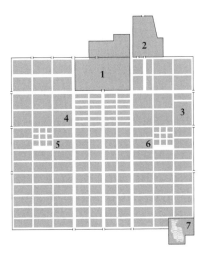

1 Imperial Palace
2 Ta Ming Palace
3 Xingqing Palace
4 Administration Area
5 West Market
6 East Market
7 Lake

Japanese patterned their plan on the Chinese capital of Changan, which had greatly impressed the Japanese diplomatic missions to the continent.

By Japanese standards Changan was a vast construction, measuring six by five miles. Basically rectangular in plan, its north-south orientation accorded with the cosmological principles of geomancy that governed the relationship of building to the forces and features of nature. The imperial palace terminated a broad central avenue that divided the city into eastern and western districts. A gridiron governed the network of major arteries and secondary streets that, in turn, directed the design of the individual courtyard house. A rampart encircled the periphery of the city; several gates punctuated the walls, allowing major streets to communicate with the countryside. The plan thus reflected imperial control, order, hierarchy of importance, and strength. In short, it represented just about everything the Japanese court wanted to be and the city it wanted to build.

Heijo-kyo (Nara) never approached Changan in either scale or completeness. The city's boundaries measured about two and two-thirds by three miles, considerably smaller than its continental prototype. The palace was centrally located, and the plan was again a gridiron. Like its mainland predecessor, the central avenue, the broadest in the city, divided the city

Heijo-kyo (Nara): Plan

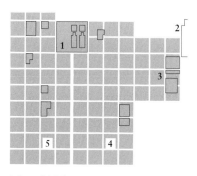

1 Imperial Palace
2 Todai-ji
3 Kofuku-ji
4 East Market
5 West Market

Heian-kyo (Kyoto): Plan

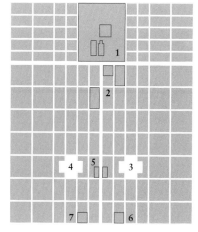

1 Imperial Palace
2 University
3 East Market
4 West Market
5 Reception Halls
6 East Temple
7 West Temple

into eastern and western districts. A market was established for each district, and temples and shrines were franchised. However, the surrounding wall remained only a plan, and while the eastern section thrived, the western district languished. Concerted efforts to remedy the situation failed to ameliorate the west's natural disadvantages such as poor soils. Bearing further testimony to the decline and eventual decay of the western sector, the current city of Nara lies well east of the original city.

In 784, Emperor Kammu moved the capital northwest to Nagaoka-kyo, a geographic location more favorable both to highway transportation and links with the port of Naniwa (today's Osaka). Here it remained, in an unfinished state, for

ten years. The city then shifted a little north and a little east and was renamed Heian-kyo, known to us today as Kyoto. Though in successive periods the seat of political power might quit the capital, the imperial residence would remain at this location for over a thousand years. Over the centuries the urban fabric of Kyoto acquired a completeness, a grace, an environment unequalled in Japan, and a sense of history that only time can cultivate.

Several reasons lay behind the establishment of the new capital, and the power of Nara's Buddhist temples is often listed as the main one. As a symbol of piety, land or land grants were donated to temples for building sites or economic holdings. Land produced rice; rice constituted wealth. And wealth bought power. In time, the temples grew in size and accumulated enormous fiscal resources. Eventually a temple such as Todai-ji could economically rival the imperial house. Buddhist influence in Nara was decisive: the church continually exerted an ever-stronger influence on the flow of politics, including one abortive attempt to have a priest installed as regent. When Kammu established Heian-kyo, he envisioned a city greater in scope, grandeur, and quality than anything Nara had offered. But with few exceptions, temples were strictly forbidden; they were expressly restricted to sites outside the city walls. And the city *was* to have walls: like the scheme for Nara, Changan provided the model for the planning of the new capital.

The natural setting of Kyoto is rich and multifaceted, having features that change constantly throughout the year. The city occupies a basin surrounded on three sides by heavily wooded hills and mountains. Two rivers, the Kamo and the Katsura, run meandering courses through the southward sloping valley floor, bringing water for agriculture and daily life. Though the city has grown over the centuries since its birth, a patchwork of open rice and vegetable fields and groves of lush green bamboo at the city's edge still exists. And the hillsides, virtually untouched by development, remain substantially wooded.

The climate of the Kyoto district is best termed variable. Though usually referred to as "mild" by most books, the stifling heat, high humidity, and heavy rains of summer create a climate with almost subtropical characteristics. Winter winds bring chillingly cold weather and often deposit a mantle of luminous snow on the surrounding hillside. Thus Kyoto tends toward the uncomfortable: hot in summer and cold in winter. Throughout the year, mists frequently envelop the mountains and their valleys, creating a vaporous beauty that has inspired generations of artists. The manmade landscape also changes with the season. Kyoto is colored from a palette of greens: deep green, light green, brilliant green, and the soft greens of mosses and algae that its moisture nurtures. The vivid green of young rice in spring matures to golden browns by the autumn's harvest. Empty and barren in winter, submerged by flooding in the spring, the paddies emerge anew in brilliant rice green by summer.

Kyoto's palette is one of greens punctuated by spots of color, often color restricted by season: spring with its whites and pinks; fall with its reds, yellows, oranges, and russets. Thus each place in Kyoto has its time, each place its color. But Kyoto is beautiful at all times of year, especially in those seasons in between: spring and autumn. In the spring, cherry blossoms tint certain of the city's districts a rosy pink. Autumn brings maple and ginkgo leaves of brightly colored hues, and gentle rains which hint at winter and the snows to come.

Even today, despite so much prosaic urban construction, the beauty of Kyoto's physical setting endures. In earlier days, we are told, the cry of animals in the forests or the sound of birds carried through the air. The landscape abounded in forests, streams, topographical features, and rich flora. However, since the eighth century—the founding of Heian-kyo —the site has never been the same. A certain formal plan definitively changed the valley for all time, and with it the history of Japan.

In terms of cosmological principles the site for Kyoto was almost ideal. There was a river flowing north-south, mountains surrounding the site on three sides, and a great mountain to the northeast, Hiei, protecting the city from evil influences. In time, numerous evil tidings did, in fact, emanate from the northeast, usually in the form of militant monks from the temple of Enryaku-ji, given special status by Kammu's order. And if geomancy regarded the site as nearly paradigmatic, so were its geographic and climatic characteristics.

The city's rectangular design measured three by three-and-a-half miles, enclosing about 6,000 acres, and was planned on the gridiron. Once again the imperial palace compound (Daidairi) was symmetrically sited at the northern edge of the city. A broad avenue extended from the southern gate northward to the palace, bisecting the city into western and eastern districts. Once again markets were established in each sector. Streets ran north-south and east-west. The main avenue measured two hundred and seventy-eight feet wide; lesser streets varied from forty feet to one hundred and seventy feet in width. The blocks resulting from the intersection of these roads, about 1,200 in all, comprised the basic neighborhood units. Each district acquired a particular character from its class and trades. The nobility, for example, settled mostly in the northwestern part of the city and the agglomeration of villas maintained the district at lower density than the central areas. By the end of the ninth century, the city was bustling with perhaps as many as 100,000 people, ten percent of whom may have been aristocrats.

Kyoto, like many cities, never fulfilled its original plan. The walls as originally conceived were left unrealized, although an earthwork of sorts surrounded the drainage canals at the city's periphery. But there was never a real need for defense, and the city walls served more to demarcate territory than to restrain an enemy. As in Nara, and in stark contrast to the rapid expansion of life and its accoutrements in the east, the western half of the city never developed. Its prosperity stagnated almost from the beginning, perhaps discouraged by the swampy quality of the soil and the periodic flooding. For centuries to come, little except a temple or stray villa occupied the lands to the west of central Kyoto. Modern Kyoto actually occupies only the eastern portion of the original plan, many of its buildings having shifted location with each rebuilding after fires or earthquakes or when the plan was revised in the sixteenth century.

Although the emperor had been careful to control the inclusion of the Buddhist institution within the city proper, certain concessions had been made. Thus, Enryaku-ji had been established on Mt. Hiei by Saicho in 788 as a sort of patron temple for the city, as well as the main temple of the then new Tendai sect. But religious sectionalism was not easily solved. In succeeding centuries violent and long-term battles ensued that often found a relatively defenseless Kyoto caught between warring religious and civil factions—with the townspeople paying the price.

Temples arose, however, but primarily beyond the city's official limits. To-ji, to the east of the main avenue and an exception to the rule, was founded in 796 as an official religious vehicle of the state. Little remains today of its former glory except its noted pagoda. In fact, little or nothing remains of anything from the Heian period within Kyoto proper, the main hall of the temple known as Sanjusangen-do, which was rebuilt in 1266 (original built in 1164), being about the oldest building extant.

Fire after fire, fire after earthquake, fire after war—all tolled the death bell for just about every structure in the city up to the sixteenth century. In 960 and again in 1180 fire virtually destroyed the city's fabric. But like the phoenix, each time Kyoto arose anew from its own ashes.

The Heian period was the golden age of Kyoto, a city created for an imperial court at its prime. Land was still plentiful; the influence and feelings of the nobility ran high. Kyoto was a new city; it was to be magnificent, this new imperial capital—unlike anything which had preceded it. The architecture assumed an elaborate guise and gardens tended toward extensive size and intricacy. It was the last time until the nineteenth century that power lay in the hands of the emperor, for shortly after the founding of the city that power was to shift into the hands of the Fujiwara regents. Neither political nor building schemes would be as complex as they were during the Heian period.

Villas and estates found sites outside the city proper. One branch of the Fujiwara family constructed its magnificent estate south of Kyoto at Uji, a district still known for its fine tea. Of the large number of buildings the estate once contained, only the Phoenix Hall of the Byodo-in survives, a delicate, birdlike structure hovering over its pond, facing the rising sun. When political power fell, so followed its architecture. Wooden structures with complex joinery and flexible infilling were easily destroyed— or disassembled and removed to another site.

Time passed. Power moved to the Taira and shortly on to the Minamotos; as if it were a political relay race, no one held the baton very long. The government moved to Kamakura in the fourteenth century but the aesthetic center of Japan remained, as it almost always would, in Kyoto. The influence of Zen and simplicity influenced the military rulers and their class and even pervaded the opulence of the court; but it was an influence, a tempering mechanism, rather than a wholesale importation of a new thought and style. With the patronage of the nobility and military Zen temples flourished, and numerous compounds arose or grew during the thirteenth and fourteenth centuries. Most of the building took place in the eastern sector, at the foot of the mountains, including the temples of Tofuku-ji (1236), Honen-in (1206), and Chion-in (1175). An exception was Tenryu-ji, founded in 1339 west of the city, at the foot of Arashiyama.

With the coming to rule of the Ashikagas, a new spotlight fell on the old capital; the sites of both emperor and shogun once again centered in Kyoto, now six centuries old. And with the shogun came other members of the military caste, who were encouraged to settle and build in Kyoto.

The craftsmen, builders, and service professionals required to support the samurai followed in their wake. Building programs were extensive. As John W. Hall writes: "Government was essentially military government, and the most impressive architectural achievements from now on were to be the product of shogunal patronage or religious inspiration."

More building took place on the fringes of the city than in the city proper, already filled to near capacity with habitations and temples that had infiltrated the urban fabric almost from the start. The semblance of order expressed in a symmetrical and carefully ordered conceptual plan evaporated. Hall continues: "A natural evolution led first to fragmentation and then to the clustering of functions by zones and belts according to the changing circumstances of government and cultural and economic activity."

Ashikaga Yoshimitsu built first his Palace of Flowers in 1378, southwest of the present palace, and then his Golden Pavilion, and withdrew to the villa in retreat from the pressures of military intrigues. By the time his grandson Yoshimasa became shogun, the civil situation had deteriorated even further. Like the image of the Amidha Buddha in his Silver Pavilion, Yoshimasa turned his back on the city and faced east, toward the hills of Higashiyama. The Onin Wars (1467–77) had erupted after long periods of famine and disease, and the city was often in flames. In the early fifteenth century Kyoto lay in relative ruin, and by century's end the population may have dropped to a low of 40,000 people. With the widespread destruction by civil war, vacant land appeared even within the central districts. By now the urban pattern was clearly established: the city continued to advance in a lopsided manner toward the east, with development spilling to the foot of the mountains like soup into a bowl.

During this period of nearly constant warfare, monasteries assumed roles as seats of learning and centers for the arts. In the mountains beyond the official city limits, temples were erected. Kiyomizu-dera, whose age nearly matches that of the city itself, was established in 798, though it was moved to the eastern hills in the early 1600s and its form as we know it dates from about 1630. Additional temples increased the density of religious institutions; Chishaku-in was established in 1598.

Villas also took to the foothills, interspersed with the temples to the east or to the northwest. Estates and villas often converted to religious institutions upon the passing of their owners, and estates changed both hands and configurations as the centuries passed. Thus Yoshimitsu commandeered the buildings and grounds of court noble Saionji Kintsune to build his Golden Pavilion; yet upon his death, the entire complex would become the temple of Rokuon-ji, more generally known as Kinkaku-ji.

In the sixteenth century—the age of consolidation: the age of Oda Nobunaga and Toyotomi Hideyoshi—Kyoto once again played a prominent role. It held its status—no matter what events transpired—as the imperial seat. Hideyoshi came to power in 1586, centralizing control of the country in a manner surpassing all those before him. His low birth and military and political training contributed little to the refinement of his taste, however. The walls of the original city plan had never materialized. Instead, Hideyoshi surrounded a good portion of Kyoto with walls following a new configuration that better reflected the state of the city—and not the idealized pattern projected at the time of the city's founding. The new plan, prepared by Maeda Genri, moved the city firmly to the east, leaving behind the atrophied western sector and including only about half of the original scheme. Roads were replotted at a considerably smaller scale than those specified on the Heian plan. The palace was relocated, and in 1591 the new earthen wall was completed. By the end of the sixteenth century the population had swelled to about a half-million inhabitants.

Hideyoshi dealt in hyperbole and extravagance: he would even try to

conquer Korea. He commissioned a
magnificent palace, the Jurakudai,
on the site of the old imperial palace
near the present Nijo Castle, only to
dismantle it several years later to
build an even more elaborate and
magnificent palace and fortifications
to replace it. Hideyoshi chose to live
outside the city, and vestiges of the
Fushimi Momoyama Castle complex
are found in temple compounds
throughout Kyoto, none more brilliant
in ornamentation and painting than
the Daishoin now at Nishi Hongan-
ji near Kyoto station. This era, the
Momoyama period, was to be Kyoto's
last grand moment. New buildings
would continue to rise, including
some magnificent and large-scale
structures, but as an environmental
ensemble, the urban composition
would never constitute comprehensive design in quite the same way.

Tokugawa Ieyasu, taking control
of Japan in 1603, shifted the capital
north and east to Edo, now known
as Tokyo. With this change in site,
Kyoto went into eclipse. Several
reasons explain the decline, but
none was more critical than the
impoverished state of the imperial
court, which became monetarily
dependent on the auspices of the
shogunate. When the homes of both
parties coincided, building projects
proceeded apace. But when their
homes graced different cities—as
they were during the Edo period—
governmental monies were normally
dispensed in places other than Kyoto.
Still, Kyoto required maintenance as

1 Imperial Palace
2 Nijo Palace
3 Jurakudai Palace
4 Outer Wall
5 Original Plan
6 Kamo River
7 Higashiyama

an administrative center for the shogunate. Thus, in 1603 the shogunate built Nijo Castle, not far from the original site of the Imperial Palace.

Unlike the hill castles of the period 1590–1610, which were primarily defensive fortifications, Nijo served entirely administrative and symbolic purposes. The need for a defensive complex, after all, had diminished to almost nil. But symbolism was always required. The fortification and its palaces were characterized by the elaborate ornamentation and excesses of the preceding Momoyama period. In style—like the Nikko shrine north of Tokyo, sacred to the memory of the first Tokugawa shogun Ieyasu—Nijo was more an example of Momoyama extravagance than of the Edo period refinement that was to follow. Nijo was the last major building project the shoguns undertook in Kyoto. With its sprawling *shoins*, concentric citadels, and lavish gardens by Kobori Enshu, it provided a fitting monument to Tokugawa power— a constant reminder to the court where the power, and the fiscal means, now lay.

Edo period courtiers wistfully recalled the halcyon days of the Heian period. In their building projects, now on a greatly reduced scale, they dealt more with reference and suggestion than with large-scale building. The imperial villas of Katsura, in the southwest,

built by Prince Toshihito, and Shugaku-in, in the northeast, created by Emperor Gomizuno, reflect a culmination of sophisticated design principles that achieve the maximum effect with a minimum of means. These works, as well as the Sento Gosho of 1634, illustrate the blossoming and fruition of environmental planning in Japan. They also represent building projects in which literary and poetic ideas, skillful use of rockwork and planting, the appreciation of yearly and eternal cycles of nature, and the relation of building to nature, coalesce into a single resolved harmony.

The late Edo period also witnessed a modification in the long-standing social structure. Merchants, traditionally assigned to the bottom of the social hierarchy, continued to amass wealth. This trend upset the former balance of money and power to some degree, and those of higher social position were forced to relinquish their aesthetic monopolies, such as those controlling the use of certain building and plant materials. Thus the merchant house and estate grew large at this time, rivaling in some instances the grandeur of the nobility.

Perry's fateful visit in the 1850s exposed the inability of the shogunate to cope with modern problems, particularly those inflicted upon Japan from the outside. The emperor called upon his shogun to expel the barbarians, but the anemic shogunate was powerless and collapsed against the threat of superior technology. Thus the shogunate fell, and in 1867 the emperor regained nominal control of the nation. Now the imperial capital was moved to Tokyo, and Kyoto accepted a role even further reduced in the life of the country.

The new government called for progress and industrialization. Although Kyoto was not affected to the same extent as Tokyo and other port cities, it too was touched by the winds of the new era. Some foreign styles intruded upon tradition, although new gardens based on the old models, such as the Murin-an by Ogawa Jihei, remained desirable. With time came streetcars, electricity, and even more ruinously, the automobile. Kyoto's atypical grid plan made mechanized transportation somewhat easier than in the complex, near-radial structures of other cities, such as castle towns. But modernization also brought problems of pollution and crowding to the somewhat fragile buildings and gardens of historical Kyoto.

Miraculously, the city survived the Pacific War relatively intact, although the continued growth of the postwar period enveloped many venerable institutions, severely modifying their original contexts. The Kyoto of today is hardly classical—in fact, the first-time visitor may be somewhat dismayed by having to search among traffic and modern buildings for the vestiges of historical places. Kyoto is a living city—a city that respects and in some way survives on its past. But it has never been closed to progress.

To date, the construction of secular projects has fortunately been restricted to the flat part of the city proper. The hills to both the east and the west, as well as those to the north, are relatively unblemished by modern urbanization. From the fumes that taint the downtown areas, a walk of fifteen to twenty minutes east to Higashiyama will allow the visitor to pass back in time several centuries. There, in the mountains, the beauty of the temples and the peacefulness of the gardens still offer considerable pleasures. Spared destruction in modern times, Kyoto still holds more historical structures and gardens than any other city in Japan. In fact, any other city in the world would have great difficulty in rivaling the wealth of Kyoto's cultural treasures or its exceptional history.

Fortunately, much remains to be seen.

Central District
Kyoto Key Map

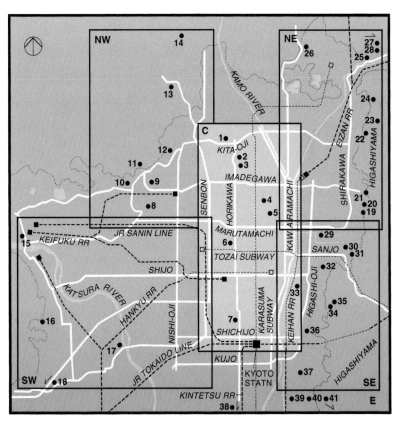

1 Daitoku-ji
2 Ura Senke
3 Omote Senke
4 Gosho
5 Sento Gosho
6 Nijo-jo
7 Nishi Hongan-ji

Central District Map

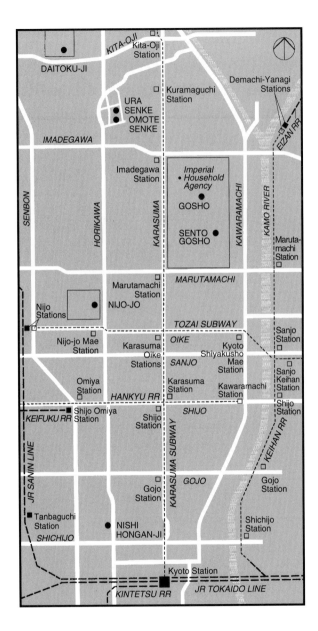

Daitoku-ji

Kita-ku, Murasakino,
Daitoku-ji-cho
Kamakura period, 1319
Rinzai Zen Buddhism
Hours: The grounds of the complex
and those temples open to the
public are generally open from
9:00 to 5:00.
Photography is permitted on the
grounds and within *some* of the
sub-temples (see individual sub-
temple entries).

Daitoku-ji, one of the largest Zen
temple precincts in Kyoto, encompasses prayer halls, additional
religious structures, and twenty-
three sub-temples possessing some
of the finest gardens in Kyoto.
Traditionally regarded as a privi-
leged place to study, the temple is
associated with many of Japan's
most famous priests, who were often
great artists and aesthetes as well
as religious figures. Rinzai sect
monasteries like Daitoku-ji were
inward-looking, walled communities
of monks practicing disciplined
personal meditation. Unlike the
grandiose Buddhist temples of earlier
sects open to the public as places of
education and charitable assistance,
Daitoku-ji remained closed to the
majority of the populace. This ex-
clusion of the outside world became
common practice in Zen compounds
in the thirteenth century.

The priest Shuho Myocho (1282–
1337), later called Daito Kokushi,
founded Daitoku-ji in 1319.
Myocho converted the emperors
Hanazono and Go-daigo to his
sect, and with imperial patronage
the temple prospered and expanded
quickly. In 1453 fire damaged the
temple, and it was destroyed completely in 1468 during the Onin
Wars. Restoration began in 1474
with imperial support, under the
direction of the priest Ikkyu.

During the sixteenth century the
temple was supported by the military government. Many sub-temples
came into being during this time, their
walled enclosures growing outward
from the formal center of the compound. Temple precincts such as
Daitoku-ji evolved over a protracted
period of time and at first glance
appear somewhat random in their
layout. Order exists, however: not
formal order in the usual sense, but
one closer to organic growth. The
compound was born, grew, died by
fire or earthquake, was reborn, and
still lives.

The planning order of Daitoku-ji
makes use of *shin-gyo-so,* or
formal, semiformal, and informal
aspects. The layout of the precinct
and its temples illustrates the transition from formal siting through
semiformal to informal planning, a
practice that has informed many of
the Japanese arts including garden
design, calligraphy (from which
the categories originally derived),
the tea ceremony, and the plans of
entire cities.

● 大徳寺　北区紫野大徳寺町

57

Entering the central area of Daitoku-ji from the south, one encounters the major buildings aligned on a north-south axis in the traditional formal manner of religious architecture in Japan and China. This is the most public zone and symbolically the most important in the precinct; the structures here are correspondingly the tallest and most massive in the temple. The walkways between the buildings run more linearly and formally than within the sub-temples and less important areas of the compound. They are also wider to accommodate processions and other religious ceremonies. Off the main walkways, gates mark entry to the sub-temples, each enclosed by high walls. Through the gate is the entry court or garden of the sub-temple; one notices the breakdown of formality almost immediately. Most paths take diagonal turns and are narrower in width than the formal walkways. The addition of smaller-scale plant materials also softens the space. These areas are the semiformal (*gyo*) spaces that form the transition between the main public spaces and the informal inner recesses of the sub-temples.

Inside, the sub-temple takes the form of a small maze of rooms connected by corridors. Interspersed within this matrix are small garden courts, verandas opening

onto serene garden scenes, and tiny linear side gardens. The sub-temples that comprise the great Kyoto Zen monasteries, such as Daitoku-ji, Myoshin-ji, Nanzen-ji and Tofuku-ji, counter the formal core of the precinct. If the central area occupies the symbolic center and visual focal point, then the sub-temple represents the center of private religious practice. More relaxed in layout, each possesses its own character and individuality, and each reflects various aspects of Zen Buddhism as practiced at Daitoku-ji from its earliest days to the present.

The main requirement for the small sub-temple is that it be conducive to contemplation and meditation, and the garden is considered paramount in the practice of the religion. The exact origin of these *kare-sansui*, or dry, gardens remains uncertain, but some evidence dates them as early as the eleventh century. Zen gardens often employed settings characterized by a deceptive simplicity, whose abstraction and symbolism may stimulate endless interpretation. To the Zen practitioner with many years of discipline these "landscapes" could transcend all physical confines. Influenced heavily by monochromatic landscape paintings of the day, many of the gardens were conceived by talented priests and artists who re-created in three dimensions scenes of varying degrees of abstraction.

Gardens for the Zen sect vary widely in style and composition, although superb craft and great elegance characterize almost all of them. Intended as remote sanctuaries for meditation, their tranquil atmosphere differs considerably from the formal, more spacious central area. These private garden worlds comprise the informal areas of the compound, yet they themselves can be further subdivided into *shin-gyo-so* styles. This complexity of design makes for endless variety.

The famous Zen priest Muso Kokushi (1271–1346) wrote at great length about the intuitive nature of gardening as opposed to "words and phrases." Muso believed one should not talk about the concepts and expressions of gardens: rather, the practice of *zazen* (seated meditation) and gardening intuitively supported enlightenment. Muso also believed that the garden of the Zen monastery is a "means by which we can give up the attachment to words and phrases and attain the ultimate reality."

At the many exquisite gardens of Daitoku-ji we can see convincing evidence of Muso's beliefs.

Note: Several of the sub-temples at Daitoku-ji are normally closed to the public except for several weeks each year. Entering any of the closed temples requires special permission from the temple office. For the serious student of gardens this is best accomplished through a Japanese national who can make a formal application, or possibly by your hotel.

1 Daisen-in
2 Koto-in
3 Koho-an
4 Hojo
5 Shinju-an
6 Ryogen-in
7 Sangen-in
8 Juko-in
9 Hoshun-in
10 Obai-in
11 Zuiho-in
12 Korin-in

Daisen-in

Muromachi period, 1509
Hours: 9:00 to 5:00 (March–November); 9:00 to 4:30 (December–February)
Photography is permitted.
Special Features: A powerful example of the dry Zen garden, creating a dramatic effect in an extremely confined space.

The Daisen-in (the Great Hermit Temple) contains one of the most photographed and celebrated gardens in Japan, a small but powerful composition of rocks and illusion. Because his landscape paintings are displayed inside the temple and because considerable design expertise guided the garden's composition, the east garden has long been attributed to Soami. Records indicate, however, that the garden was laid out by the temple founder Kogaku Shuko (1464–1548), but it is not unlikely that Soami collaborated on the project at some point.

The garden occupies a narrow strip of ground some twelve feet wide by forty-seven feet long. Surely one of the finest three-dimensional miniaturizations of an idealized landscape scene in Japan, it was realized in the tradition of Chinese paintings of the Song period (960–1279). The Song manner greatly

Daisen-in: Detail of east garden

大仙院　北区紫野大徳寺町（大徳寺山内）

influenced Muromachi period painters and garden designers, and the east garden abstracted and translated into garden form paintings of vast cliffs and falling waters.

The carefully scaled trees, shrubs, and rocks portray a mountain grouping with cascading "water" that flows continuously under bridges, around and between islands, over a dam, finally exiting the garden beneath the building. The exquisitely refined placement of the rocks contributes significantly to the overall believability of the landscape vision.

The focus in the lower (south) part of this small scene is a remarkable boat-shaped rock that once belonged to the shogun Ashikaga Yoshimasa (1435–1490). A plaster wall/bridge with a bell-shaped opening—constructed as recently as 1961—bisects the garden. This controversial move has led some critics to comment on the disturbance of visual movement through the entire scene, but there is some indication that a bridge of this sort did exist at one time during the garden's history. Prints of the garden dating to the seventeenth century show no evidence of the wall, however.

In addition to the principal garden area, a second garden occupies the south side of the Hojo. It consists of a large rectangle of sand with two sand piles set upon it and is typical of *hojo* gardens of this period (see Daitoku-ji Hojo). Additional gardens bracket the two remaining

sides of the temple. They are well crafted but of little historical note.

Comments: Daisen-in is the most visited of the temples at Daitoku-ji and is on the commercial tourist circuit. It receives hoards of people, including schoolchildren taking tours in Kyoto. Centrally located and highly popular, the garden may be crowded to excess. It is best to wait for lulls between groups or to visit very early to truly enjoy the splendid east garden.

Daisen-in: The east garden

Koto-in ∎

Momoyama period, c. 1603
Hours: 9:00 to 4:30
Photography is permitted.

Koto-in, one of the smaller Daitoku-ji temples, was founded by Hosokawa Tadaoki (1563–1645), a noted Momoyama-period warrior. Entering the precinct is an instructive and moving spatial experience. After passing through the main gate, one follows a path that turns and continues along a handsome stone walkway. The maple trees flanking both sides of the walk form a delicately leafed canopy that filters the sunlight in a textured pattern on the ground. At the end of the walk a second gate, featuring a small bell-shaped window with *shoji*, terminates the view. On occasion the window is left open—allowing a peek into the garden beyond—but one cannot actually enter the garden through this gate. After offering this tantalizing glimpse the path again turns right, then left, and finally leads to the temple entry. (See Ginkaku-ji for a related entry sequence.)

A grove of maple trees also shades the garden south of the Hojo (Superior's Quarters). Moss coats parts of the earthen surface; a single stone lantern stands as the garden's focal point. In another area, a finely contrived path (*roji*) leads to the teahouse named Shoko-ken. Koto-in's numerous maples burst into stunning color in the autumn, but the garden is normally bathed in tranquility. While not nearly as famous as other gardens in Daitoku-ji, the Koto-in has its own unique qualities and excellence of design. Since this garden is rarely crowded, it is a serene place to sit and enjoy the passing of time and the delicacy of nature.

Koto-in: The south garden

● 高桐院　北区紫野大徳寺町（大徳寺山内）

63

Koho-an

Edo period, 1621
Hours: Not open to the general public; special permission is required.
Photography is not permitted.

Koho-an is a temple rich in gardens and architectural refinement. Several of the gardens were designed by the noted landscape architect Kobori Enshu (1579–1647), whose hand can be seen in these landscapes renowned for their originality and superb layout.

This temple is organized in a manner quite different from earlier temples at Daitoku-ji, such as the Shinju-an and the Hojo. In these other temples each room opens onto the next, and to exterior spaces as well; corridors extend along the perimeter and through the buildings, acting as connective and structuring elements. At Koho-an, however, the planning so skillfully juxtaposes room and corridor that they read as a single entity. As a result, the gardens appear to merge with interior spaces, and the gardens surround the buildings while being surrounded by them. The movable exterior partitions transform into internal divisions or disappear entirely.

The garden belonging to the room called the Bosen is a striking example of Enshu's design skill and the incorporation of a literary idea into an architectural space.

This room, an interior tearoom, departs from the more usual reference to the teahouse as a rustic cottage approached from the garden path. Here the literary metaphor was the "boat at sea." One enters the room along a narrow corridor that alludes to a boat docked on a shoreline. Only when seated in the tearoom (or the "interior" of the boat) does a view beyond the veranda open into the garden—visible below an unusual *shoji* screen that slides vertically. The low-hanging *shoji* also forces the view downwards to the small foreground garden, whose large hedge serves as its rear wall. This hedge, however, screens only about one-half of the scene, permitting Enshu to cleverly "borrow" landscape elements from the garden beyond. The visual extension of the garden creates a feeling of intimacy and expansiveness simultaneously.

The garden off the Hojo is the more common large and flat rectangle of moss. A double hedge encloses the garden and may allude to the waves of the sea, a popular literary metaphor in Enshu's gardens. Placing yourself at sea, or viewing one of the noted Japanese or Chinese shorelines while meditating, was considered fitting Zen practice and often used as a formal metaphor in garden design.

A larger garden, more pictorial in its representation of the landscape, lies beyond the Bosen area. Essentially a flat garden of earth, moss, and rocks, it is a scene containing water and promontories with an arched bridge and background plantings. In the winter, the fallen needles of the surrounding pine trees often carpet the bare earth, a texture that adds a poignant dimension to a superb garden.

In summation, Koho-an, a tribute to Enshu's genius, exemplifies the practice of maximizing limited space and achieving great complexity with only simple parts. The formal entry to the temple also warrants note for its exceptional stone walkway, composed of alternating rectangular and rounded stones, a masterpiece in itself. Several other gardens, among the finest at Daitoku-ji, can also be found at Koho-an.

Koho-an: View from the Bosen

Daitoku-ji Hojo
Superior's Quarters

Edo period, present buildings 1636
Hours: Not usually open to the
public; special permission is required.
Photography is not permitted.

The Daitoku-ji Hojo, a designated
national treasure, exemplifies a
layout common to many sub-temples
in Zen precincts of the period.
Within the overall scheme, the
arrangements and sizes of the
buildings vary, but the temples
themselves share basic physical
similarities (see plan).

The layout usually consists of a
main building (called the *Hojo*)
containing reception rooms and
a memorial chapel, and other
structures that include the living
quarters for the monks, kitchens,
storage rooms, and often a teahouse. Gardens surround the buildings within these walls: fruit and
vegetable gardens in the rear areas,
ornamental contemplative gardens
adjacent to the main buildings.
Covered corridors weave the many
structures of the temple into a single
fabric, the arrangement of the buildings determined by function and
orientation. The structures often
exhibit formal and geometric relationships while the gardens soften the
stricture of these walled enclosures.

The Daitoku-ji Hojo contains gardens
to the east and south sides of the
building, which date to the reloca-
tion of the building in 1636. The

south, and principal, garden reflects
a type of hojo garden found at
many Zen temples. Its form consists
of a rectangle of raked gravel, edged
by low shrubs and enclosed by a
white plaster wall. Carefully positioned trees and shrubs trimmed
into a variety of rounded shapes
mute the stark lines of the walls.
Several rocks and two sand mounds
articulate the gravel area. Found in
many hojo gardens, these mounds
are said to symbolize mountains or
islands originally associated with
Buddhist doctrine. Others believe
they refer to famous mountains in
China or Japan. The origin of the
mounds probably derives, in fact,
from either Shinto practice or
storage heaps of gravel used in the
garden that were incorporated as
both design and metaphorical
elements at some point in time.

The east Hojo garden, while a
separate entity, visually merges at
its south extreme with the principal garden. It is essentially a
narrow plot with shrubs, sand, and
rock arrangements, and is traditionally attributed to Kobori Enshu.
Originally this was a "borrowed
scenery" garden with a splendid
view of the distant Kamo river with
Mt. Hiei composed as the main
element of the design. Now blocked
by the adjacent buildings, the effect
has been considerably lessened.

1

2

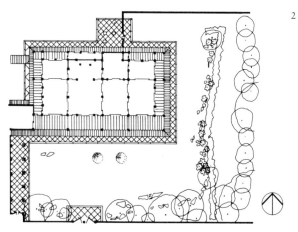

Daitoku-ji Hojo
1 The south garden gravel mounds
2 Plan

67

Shinju-an

Muromachi period, 1491
Hours: Not usually open to the public; special permission is required.
Photography is not permitted.

Shinju-an was founded in honor of the highly esteemed priest Ikkyu, abbot of Daitoku-ji from 1474–1481. The Hojo's (Superior's Quarters) south and east gardens are attributed to Murata Shuko, a famous tea master, under the patronage of the shogun Ashikaga Yoshimasa (see Ginkaku-ji).

To the south, a dry garden substitutes a carpet of moss, added in the seventeenth century, for the more standard raked gravel. Except for the border hedges, few other plants intrude on this central field. Within its confines stands a single pine tree placed off-center, thought to have been inspired by the famous Zen koan: "What is the meaning of the Buddha-mind?" One of the acceptable answers: "A single pine tree growing in a garden."

East of the Hojo lies the most noted garden at Shinju-an, although it was reduced in size in 1601. Moss was encouraged to grow as a groundcover some time thereafter. The stone arrangement in this garden also warrants the visitor's attention. Here Shuko arranged fifteen rocks in a beautiful 7-5-3 cluster pattern, utilizing the auspicious "harmony of odd numbers" inspired by Chinese principles of arrangement and widely used in the Japanese arts.

Today we see the three rock groupings, each an odd-numbered composition, emerging from a sea of moss. Behind the ground plane stands a three-foot-high backdrop hedge, with maple trees placed at random intervals behind it. In summer, the trees form a shady canopy that filters light and peppers the garden with shadows. In the fall, leaves turn a myriad of colors; in the winter, the absence of leaves allows more light to penetrate into this confined area. The skill of working in tight spaces without sacrificing quality or richness and the concern for the quality of light is particularly evident in this garden.

A rustic teahouse augmented the collection of structures at Shinju-an in 1638. The *roji*, or approach, to the teahouse consists of a curving path of stepping stones designed to suggest a rural mountain path. The tea ceremony became closely associated with Zen and entered the teaching at Daitoku-ji in the late fifteenth century under Ikkyu. The teahouse and its entry garden, like the other gardens at Shinju-an, reflect the attitude of leaving the everyday world for the realm of religious and aesthetic objectives.

真珠庵

北区紫野大徳寺町（大徳寺山内）

68

Ryogen-in

Muromachi period, c. 1504
Hours: 9:00 to 4:30
Photography is permitted.

This temple founded by Tokei Soboku boasts five gardens of various sizes. It claims the smallest garden in Japan (Totekiko), as well as the oldest (Ryugin-tei) in the Daitoku-ji complex. The main garden has been attributed to Soami, although this assignment has not been definitively established. The garden known as Isshidan was refurbished in the 1980s with forms stronger in definition and profile than those executed in a more historical manner. The islands and rock arrangements symbolize the themes of the crane and tortoise as well as the mythical Chinese Mt. Horai.

Ryogen-in: The Isshidan garden renewed

Some other gardens at Daitoku-ji

Obai-in

Momoyama period, 1588
Hours: Not open to the public except once a year in the fall; special permission is required at all other times.
Photography is permitted.

Korin-in

Muromachi period, 1533
Hours: Not open to the public except twice a year; special permission is required at all other times.
Photography is permitted.

Zuiho-in   ■

Muromachi period, 1541 (gardens, Shigemori Mirei, 1960s)
Hours: 9:00 to 5:00
Photography is permitted.

Juko-in

Muromachi period, 1582
Hours: Not open to the public except twice a year; special permission is required at all other times.
Photography is not permitted.

Sangen-in

Momoyama period, 1589
Hours: Not open to the general public.
Photography is not permitted.

Hoshun-in

Momoyama period, c. 1608
Hours: Not usually open to the public; special permission is required.
Photography is not permitted.

●

龍源院

北区紫野大徳寺町（大徳寺山内）

Ura Senke

Kamigyo-ku, Honpojimae-cho
Momoyama period
Hours: Not usually open to the
public; special permission is required.
Photography is not permitted.

Ura Senke, among the most celebrated schools of the tea ceremony,
traces its origins to one of the most
famous tea masters of all time, Sen
no Rikyu (1520–1591). Today a
prospering institution with branches
in many countries, Ura Senke is
headed by Sen Soshitsu, a sixteenth-
generation descendant of Rikyu.
The grounds of the school contain
many fine teahouses and gardens.

Characterizing tea gardens in
general, it can be said that they
differ from most types of Japanese
gardens in that their primary function
is to provide a modest approach to
the teahouse, rather than a setting
for the tea ceremony itself. The
garden is as much the actual walk
or movement through the space as
the physical elements of which it
is comprised. Often likened to a
rural path leading to a rustic hut
in the woods, the tea garden (*roji*)
aspired to be unassuming, to nurture
rather than detract from the main
subject, the tea ceremony.
(See also Koetsu-ji.)

The influence of the tea garden
became widespread during the
Edo period. Following a path that
led from the quotidian world to that
of the timeless mood of tea, one
moved along a predetermined route
whose views as well as features of
visual interest were carefully controlled. The ubiquitous stepping
stones are thought to have been first
used functionally in tea gardens, to
elevate the visitor from muddy
paths as well as to guide movement.
Lanterns also had functional origins,
to light the way for ceremonies
held at dusk or after dark. The elements and principles of the tea garden found their way into the large
stroll gardens of the Edo period,
although at a scale greatly expanded
for intentions more secular than the
almost religious mood of tea.

The Ura Senke gardens well illustrate these philosophical and design
ideas and offer an appropriate setting to study the architecture and
gardens of tea.

裏千家 上京区小川通寺之内上ル

Omote Senke

Kamigyo-ku, Honpojimae-cho
Momoyama period
Hours: Not usually open to the
public; special permission is required.
Photography by permission.

Omote Senke, like Ura Senke, is a
tea ceremony school with origins
related to the tea master Sen no
Rikyu (1520–1591). Rikyu's grandson,
Sotan, divided the house of Sen
among three of his sons. One founded
the Mushanokoji Senke school of
tea; a second son was given the back
part of the property (Ura Senke);
and a third, the front (Omote Senke).
All three schools have continued to
prosper to this day.

The grounds of the Omote Senke
school include several teahouses
and tea gardens of high quality
(see Ura Senke for an explanation
of the tea garden). Both Omote
and Ura Senke maintain important
examples of such gardens for those
interested in the tea ceremony.

●
表千家

上京区小川通寺之内上ル

Ura Senke: View of the tea garden

Kyoto Gosho
Kyoto Imperial Palace

Kamigyo-ku, Kyoto Gyoen
Edo period, completed 1790;
present buildings 1855

Hours: Visitors can obtain permission to tour the Imperial Palace from the office of the Imperial Household Agency located on the palace grounds. The palace is open on weekdays; Saturdays in April, May, October, and November; and the third Saturday of the other months. It is closed on national holidays and from 28 December to 4 January. Tours start at 10:00 and 2:00 and last about one hour. The Gosho is also opened two times a year to the general public, for one week in April and again in October. At these times, however, the grounds are extremely crowded.

Photography is permitted.

The Kyoto Imperial Palace today reflects but faintly the architectural styles and layout of its Heian period ancestor. The original palace, built in 794, was located southwest of the present site, near what is today Nijo Castle, but warfare and numerous fires repeatedly destroyed its structures. The palace was moved to its present location about 1788, but even there the fires that plagued Kyoto still troubled its monumental pavilions. The buildings that now occupy the grounds date from 1855. While the intent in this last rebuilding was to preserve Heian styles, only the flavor of the early architecture, and the *shinden-zukuri* (*shinden* style) layout, color the architecture. Over the centuries, repeated reconstructions slowly changed the scale and style of the original buildings, departing considerably from the original models. The Gosho does, however, exude a sense of the stately, formal planning and sumptuous interiors of Japanese palace architecture that has existed through the centuries.

The primary element among the palace's buildings is the ceremonial hall (Shishinden) and the enclosed courtyard to its south. Only two elements intrude upon this austere yet elegant plane of raked gravel: an orange tree and a cherry tree that flank the stairs of the hall. This courtyard, typical of those found in early palaces, served religious and official ceremonies and derived from the cleared area (*yuniwa*) of Shinto shrines. It is thought that as the early court became more concerned with festivity than religious ceremony, plants, trees, and ponds gradually entered these spaces with increasing concentrations until they had become the original palace gardens. This change in the use of outdoor space may also have reflected the increasing worldliness of the nobility, who attempted to re-create within their own enclaves points of interest seen on their travels. Today, this courtyard at the Shishinden retains hints of Heian and earlier palace planning, however pale.

京都御所　上京区京都御苑

72

In addition to the palace buildings and courtyard, a second garden may be seen on the tour. Sited east of the Kogosho building is a large pond garden known as Oike-no-niwa; not closely related to its surrounding buildings, it too bears little resemblance to its Heian predecessor. Its last reconstruction dates from the late Edo period.

Sento Gosho
Retired Emperor's Villa

■

Kamigyo-ku, Kyoto Gyoen
Edo period, 1634

Hours: The villa is open for tours on weekdays; Saturdays in April, May, October, and November; and the third Saturday of the other months. It is closed on national holidays and from 28 December to 4 January. Tours last approximately one hour. Visitors must secure advance permission from the Kyoto office of the Imperial Household Agency located on the grounds of the Old Imperial Palace (Gosho). It is important to be on time as tours start promptly.

Photography is permitted.

Special Features: One of the most sophisticated examples of the stroll garden type.

The Sento Gosho, the principal residence of the retired Emperor Gomizuno (1596–1680), is one of three imperial villas—the others being Katsura and Shugaku-in—still extant in Kyoto. Originally built in the early 1600s, the buildings of the palace were destroyed by fire in 1708, rebuilt, and burned down again for the last time in 1854. Originally a wall divided the garden into north and south sections, destined as individual villas for emperor and empress. The wall was removed in the mid 1700s, at which time additional strolling paths were configured. In the garden's early days, its sizable ponds supported boating activities, but when the two gardens were unified

Kyoto Gosho: The enclosed forecourt

●

仙洞御所

上京区京都御苑

the emphasis changed to a more representative stroll garden.

The making of Sento Gosho brought together the talents of Emperor Gomizuno and landscape architect Kobori Enshu. Holding no real political power at this time, the emperor had ample opportunity for aesthetic interests. A devout Zen practitioner, he was also knowledgeable in many of the arts of the day. Enshu, a government magistrate, possessed a brilliant intellect and was himself an accomplished tea master, Zen priest, and designer.

Working with a team of relatives and associates, Enshu designed and realized palaces and gardens for the nobility, and his influence was felt far beyond the handful of gardens attributed to him. A clever innovator, Enshu ably combined the elegance of the court style with the austerity required by the tea ceremony and Zen. The aristocrats for whom he designed lived an almost sequestered and powerless life, yet aspired to the ways of bygone eras such as the Heian period. By combining a variety of simple and elegant styles, Enshu provided them with at least the illusion of the grandeur of the older estates. The nobility's rejection of the ornamentation and polychrome that characterized the residences of the shogunate was itself an attempt to set themselves aesthetically apart —and perhaps even above—the military rulers of the nation.

Today the Sento Gosho remains a superb example of the stroll garden. Used and modified by retired emperors and gardeners through the centuries, its design, through movement and a series of unexpected sights, reveals startling surprises and visual delights. Dynamic and ever-changing, its experience is visually and haptically kinetic.

At Sento Gosho, the pathways assume far simpler forms than those at the Katsura Villa, and the garden seems restrained by comparison— although it lacks none of its imperial elegance. One might easily imagine gliding across the ponds in brightly colored boats with carved dragon bows. As on foot, the views would have been constantly transformed; pleasant surprises waited around the bend of the various islands, making for a charming journey. Along the way, a pavilion offered rest or the enjoyment of a particularly fine vista. Sento Gosho and Katsura share the same aesthetic goal: each presents an idealized landscape with a variety of scenes and vistas along paths that cohere as a total artistic experience.

Sento Gosho was built for an emperor without political power, but an emperor who nonetheless remained the tutelary symbol of the state. The garden therefore exhibits a quality of extreme repose that lies beyond worldly power, a repose of serene and understated beauty.

Comments: Of particular note is the cobblestone beach (*ariso*), the symbolic representation of a natural coastline and gift of the lord of the Odawara clan in eastern Japan. It is commonly believed that the stones were gathered in Odawara and individually wrapped in silk for transport to Kyoto and presentation to the emperor. They were known as "two liter stones," for each was said to have the value at the time of two liters of rice.

Sento Gosho
1 Garden paths direct movement and view
76 2 The *ariso* beach

Nijo-jo
Nijo Castle ■

Nakagyo-ku, Nijo-jo-cho
Momoyama period, 1603;
renovated Edo period, 1624–1626
Hours: 8:45 to 5:00 (last entry 4:00);
closed from 26 December to
4 January.
Photography is permitted.

Nijo Castle was built by Ieyasu, the first of the Tokugawa shoguns, as an administrative center and symbol of power. Construction of the stately buildings that served as the shogun's residence was completed in 1603 while the Fushimi Momoyama Castle south of Kyoto remained the headquarters of the state. When Edo (present-day Tokyo) became the political center of the nation, Nijo Castle was used only when the shogun made a rare visit to the old capital. After the shogunate was overthrown in 1867, Nijo Castle became an imperial villa; in 1939, it became the property of the city of Kyoto.

In 1624 construction expanded the buildings and renovated the garden, ordered by the third Tokugawa shogun Iemitsu (1604–1651) in preparation for a visit by Emperor Gomizuno (1596–1680). The celebrated landscape designer and tea master Kobori Enshu supervised the work on the gardens.

The historical garden at Nijo Castle lies to the southwest of the palace and the *shoin* buildings that comprise the Ninomaru citadel, all of which were completely refurbished for the imperial visit. In addition, a special new palace called the Gyoku Goten was built as a temporary residence for the emperor; but this palace, connected to the Ninomaru by covered corridors, was dismantled shortly after Gomizuno's visit.

The buildings at Nijo are resplendent with carved and painted ornamentation and exemplify the power of the Tokugawa regime to concentrate the era's greatest artists on a single building project. In strong contrast to this self-conscious architectural display, the refined imperial villa at Katsura expresses the disenfranchised nobility's embrace of simple yet elegant materials.

The garden at Nijo, approximately one acre in size, has undergone many alterations over the centuries. Its composition centers on a large pond containing several islands and numerous groupings of stones and plantings. Some historians have speculated that the garden was originally planned without trees and the pond without water, to affect the look of a "dry garden." Old photos, in fact, do show the pond left dry, exposing a pebbled bottom, and much of the plant material does seem more recent than Enshu's refurbishing. There is, however, no substantiation for the idea that these effects were a part of the original design or were intended to be left in their dry form.

二条城　中京区二条城町

1

While it is possible to walk through areas of the garden, the best views are obtained from within the buildings. Unlike the design of the Katsura landscape—where the garden setting carefully enfolds the villa and walks lead through a series of separate unfolding scenes—the Nijo garden is not closely related to the Ninomaru structures. The garden is more likely a holdover from the Momoyama period; and one might easily imagine the ephemeral palace built for the emperor's visit, in conjunction with the other buildings, totally enclosing the garden space as if a courtyard.

From the rooms and veranda of the shoins one may best enjoy the perfected scene that this garden represents. Many of the rocks are

of enormous size, which lends some credence to the supposition that the garden was to be viewed from a distance. Rather than achieving more subtle effects with less elaborate resources—a practice that characterized the making of the Katsura and Shugaku-in imperial villas—the Nijo garden above all reads as an artistic grouping of plants (including rare cycads), water, and massive stones—all to express Tokugawa presence.

2

3

Nijo Castle
1 Garden with *shoin* beyond
2 Pond with island landscape
3 Rock, pine, and water

Nishi Hongan-ji

Shimogyo-ku, Monzen-cho
Momoyama period, 1591
Headquarters of the Hongan-ji
School of Shinshu Buddhism
(Jodo-Shinshu)

Hours: Tours of the Daishoin
including the Kokei-no-niwa are
available daily at 10:45 and 2:45.
Prior confirmation is recommended.
Commentary is in Japanese only.

Photography is not permitted in
the Daishoin—garden photos
usually permitted.

Special Features: The Daishoin
Hall and the Karamon Gate, both
"national treasures," are among
the finest examples of Momoyama
architecture. The Kokei-no-niwa
is a superbly composed garden
featuring cycads as its principal
plant specimens.

Nishi Hongan-ji was founded in
1272 at Higashiyama as the main
temple of the Jodo-Shinshu sect.
It was moved to its present site in
1591 when Toyotomi Hideyoshi
donated land for new construction.
The temple precinct contains several
structures of historical and architectural interest including the Hondo,
or Main Hall (reconstructed in 1760),
and the Daishido, or Founder's
Hall, built in 1636.

To the rear, that is, the west, of
the buildings is the Daishoin Hall,
which was re-erected here in 1632
after the dissolution of Hideyoshi's
Fushimi Momoyama Castle. One

of the most superb pieces of Momoyama architecture extant, it proffers
a magnificent array of Kano school
fusuma (opaque sliding panels)
paintings.

The Kokei-no-niwa, or "Tiger-glen"
garden is situated to the east, between the Daishoin and the new
temple office. The garden merits
attention for at least two reasons:
the presence of cycads, a palmlike
gymnosperm of tropical origin and
relatively rare in Japan, and the
absence of pine trees, a species almost
requisite in any Japanese garden.

The garden is intended to be seen
from the veranda or the interior of
the Daishoin. Its composition
possesses a sense of symmetry
although not strictly symmetrical.
Two round pruned trees toward
the left balance trees set to the
right; the two islands, although
placed off-center in the central
space, are linked by stone bridges
that connect them with the rear
grouping of plants. Executed in the
kare-sansui (dry) garden style,
the Kokei-no-niwa uses larger
and darker stones in the foreground composition with a white
gravel cover over the remainder
of the ground surface. Several
rocks, which also anchor the foreground of the composition, separate
the garden's mineral and vegetal
areas.

This garden conveys a feeling of
relative stasis: composed, in equilibrium. As a tableau, though beautiful,

it keeps the viewer outside the garden space and firmly on the veranda.
Unlike a garden such as Ryoan-ji,
where continued viewing and introspection reveals new depths of
thought, the Kokei-no-niwa reveals
only more details of its making.
In the tradition of the Momoyama
arts, its beauty and its richness
delight the senses rather than engage
the mind to provoke contemplation.

Northwest District
Kyoto Key Map

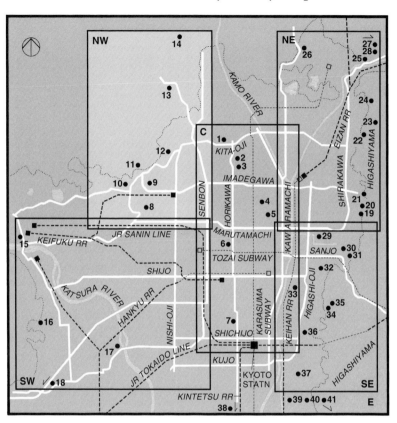

Northwest District Map

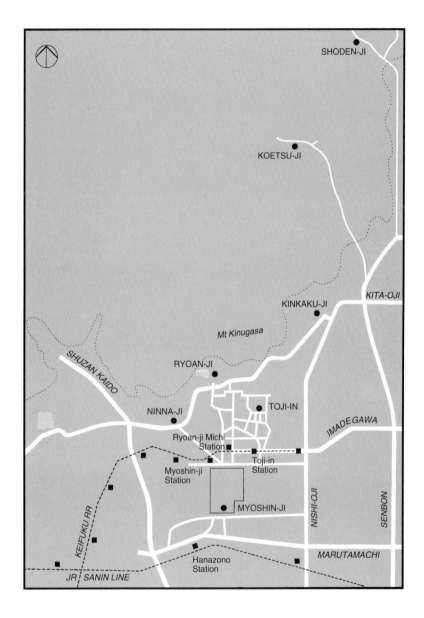

Myoshin-ji

Ukyo-ku, Hanazono,
Myoshin-ji-cho
Kamakura period, founded 1337
Headquarters of the Myoshin-ji
school of Rinzai Zen Buddhism

Hours: The grounds are open daily.
See individual sub-temples for
their hours.

Photography is permitted on the
grounds and within some of the
sub-temples.

Myoshin-ji—with Daitoku-ji,
Nanzen-ji, and Tofuku-ji—composes
one of the major Zen temple
precincts in the Kyoto area. Built
additively over the centuries, the
compound includes prayer halls,
religious structures, and numerous
sub-temples, and employs typical
Zen temple precinct planning (see
Daitoku-ji). The temple grounds
occupy the site of the former villa of
Kiyowara Natsuno (782–837); it
later became a retirement villa for
the Emperor Hanazono (ruled
1308–1318), who in turn gave the
land to the priest Egen (Kanzan
Kokushi) in 1337. Egen founded
Myoshin-ji in that year and around
1350 became its first abbot.

The sub-temples of Myoshin-ji are
rich in artistic treasures. Gardens
are numerous as well, and although
not as notable as those of Daitoku-
ji, many possess their own individual merits. These gardens provide
secluded sanctuaries for meditation
and mirror the refined simplicity

and beauty that has long been associated with the practice and ethics
of Zen Buddhism.

Note: Many of the sub-temples at
Myoshin-ji are normally closed to
the public; others open their doors
only annually. To enter those
normally closed requires special
permission from the temple office.
For the serious student of gardens
this is best done through a Japanese
national who can present a formal
application. Hotels, or the city
tourist office, may be of assistance
in securing permission.

●
妙心寺　右京区花園妙心寺町

Taizo-in ■

Muromachi period
Hours: 9:00 to 5:00
Photography is permitted.

The garden of the Taizo-in represents the Muromachi Zen landscape as a pictorial composition;
in essence, it could be likened to
a painting translated into three
dimensions. A balanced, yet
dynamic, composition of angular
rocks gives the impression of steep
cliffs, with a particularly effective
use of small cobbles to suggest a
watercourse. Background foliage
creates a forested effect, while a
horizontal plane of white gravel
weaves through the rocks, creating
the illusion of a much larger scene.

Here, as in most dry gardens, we
see nature's scenery reduced and
abstracted. But though nature is
compressed within these diminutive
confines, it is at the same time
expanded, giving the impression of
a greater universe. Through meditation and the intimate relation of the
monk to the garden the bounded
space evaded its limits. As a part of
the intense training integral to Zen,
monks diligently maintained the
gardens; through the intense concentration demanded by contemplative practices they freed their minds
from the everyday world.

Taizo-in has long been associated
with the Kano school of painting
and, in fact, Kano Motonobu
(1475–1559) lived at Myoshin-ji

for some time. The name of the
builder of the Taizo-in garden
remains obscure, but its form bears
some similarities to the Kano
style: the strong angular lines and
the realism of its elements present
a more readily grasped landscape
scene than other Zen gardens, such
as Ryoan-ji or Reiun-in. These
other gardens are more abstract
than Taizo-in and their elements
imply more than depict the physical
landscape.

A recent garden by Nakane Kinsaku
complements the historical courtyard
landscape: much larger in scale than
the usual Zen garden, it is also a
landscape in which to walk. Although
not a stroll garden in the strict sense
(see Katsura and Sento Gosho), it
relates more closely to that type than
to the classic dry gardens meant to
be seen from a fixed viewpoint
removed from the actual garden space.
This new garden, while lacking both
a sense of history and a clearly stated
idea, is handsome in composition
and its sloped carpet of azaleas. It is
best seen from its far end, looking
back across the water and rocks to
the greenery beyond, particularly in
springtime when pink blossoms
sparkle as if illuminated from within.

● 退蔵院 右京区花園妙心寺町（妙心寺山内）

86

1

2

Taizo-in
1 The Muromachi garden
2 The modern garden by Nakane Kinsaku

Reiun-in

Muromachi period, founded 1526; garden c. 1543
Hours: Not usually open to the public; special permission is required.
Photography by permission.

The Reiun-in temple is known for the painter Kano Motonobu's (1475–1559) residence there, and the numerous paintings by the artist it contains. The temple's notable garden—which lies to the south of the *shoin*'s Gorinko room—was believed to be coeval with the new shoin, built especially for an imperial visit around 1543.

A small strip of land approximately ten by thirty feet in dimension foregrounds a wall of unique design that extends along its full length. The white horizontal bands in the plaster are said to indicate imperial distinction bestowed upon the temple. A simple dry garden of several rock groupings and pruned shrubs lies before this wall. Attributed to the priest Shiken Seido, the garden is more abstract in its imagery than the garden of nearby Taizo-in, its principal focus being the composition of upright and horizontal rocks to the eastern side.

Pleasing in effect, this small, enclosed, and often shaded garden feels like a most suitable place for meditation.

Gyokuho-in

Momoyama period
Hours: Not usually open to the public; special permission is required.
Photography by permission.

The sub-temple of Gyokuho-in is best known as the first residence of Emperor Hanazono after his abdication. Little of the original architecture remains, however, and the origins of the gardens are obscure.

The garden south of the temple buildings is rather unorthodox, yet satisfying nonetheless. A dry garden of large proportions, its simple design grants it a certain elegance. Formal walkways of rectangular stones traverse a lengthy bed of raked gravel, occasionally punctuated by a large tree that adds just sufficient verticality to counter the dominant horizontal thrust. Enclosed by buildings on one side and plaster walls on the others, this carefully contrived garden demonstrates the skill with which the Japanese gardener created complete landscape worlds within the strictures of severely limited spaces. Still visible on one wall are the white horizontal plaster bands that denote imperial benefaction—also found at Reiun-in.

● 霊雲院 妙心寺

● 玉鳳院 妙心寺

88

Toji-in

Kita-ku, Toji-in, Kitamachi
Kamakura period, founded 1341;
present structures rebuilt in 1818.
Tenryu-ji school of Rinzai
Zen Buddhism
Hours: 8:00 to 5:00
Photography is permitted.
Special Features: A hill and pond
garden that displays the calming
influence of tea in its materials
and form.

One would expect that any building
project undertaken by the Ashikaga
family would be characterized by
refinement and dignity, and at Toji-in
both appear in abundance. Its garden displays a concise and precise
composition of both hill and pond
garden elements that together
maintain a delicate beauty year-round.

The temple was founded by Ashikaga Takauji in 1341 and served
as the familial temple for fifteen
subsequent Ashikaga shoguns.
The feeling of the garden suggests little of the turbulent times
that bred the great Onin Wars of
the 1460s, when the shogunate ruled
from the Muromachi district of
Kyoto. Characteristic of the period,
and in contrast to the political
troubles, was the delicate atmosphere
of the garden's aesthetic: the careful
yet informal layout of planting,
water, and rockwork. The garden
is usually attributed to Muso

Toji-in: View of garden and tea house

等持院

北区等持院北町

Kokushi, but there is little evidence of his hand, and numerous changes in the garden have obscured any character of the Kamakura period.

The principal feature of the eastern section is a pond in the form of the Japanese character *shin*, meaning heart or spirit, 心, also used at Saiho-ji. This part of the garden was rebuilt in modern times by Nakane Kinsaku and focuses on the "lotus" pond and the teahouse Seiren-tei, added later by Ashikaga Yoshimasa. A stone bridge leads to the central island meant to recall the island of Horai from Chinese antiquity, while many fine compositions of rockwork ring the pond. A complex arrangement of bushes, clipped hedges, stones, and paths gracefully connects the two levels.

The veranda of the temple provides a fine view of the two ponds and lush greenery within the garden. To the left, the intricate texture of the planted slope leads the eye uphill to the Seiren-tei. Unfortunately, Mt. Kinugasa, whose beauty prompted the building of the temple, is no longer visible in the distance: today, the buildings of a college campus abut the temple grounds and blunt the vista.

Toji-in remains a very special garden, distinct from its siblings in and around Kyoto. Within a very compact space, its finely resolved composition of garden elements offers the visitor a peaceful experience removed from traffic and commerce. Fortunately, it is located just far enough from the tourist path to retain a sense of calm unspoiled by the noise and presence of large numbers of people.

Comments: Although Toji-in is agreeable at any time of day, it projects a particular beauty in the late afternoon, when the highlights are dramatic and the shadows deep. The camellias and azaleas bloom in the spring, and the *mokusei* (*Osmanthus fragrans*) turn to bright color in the fall, punctuating the green texture of the planting with points of intense color.

Toji-in: Clipped shrubs and rock groupings

Ninna-ji

Ukyo-ku, Omuro, Ouchi
Heian period, completed 886;
present buildings and gardens,
early Edo period.
Headquarters of the Omuro school
of Shingon Buddhism.
Hours: 9:00 to 4:00
Photography is permitted.
Special Features: A waterfall and
pond are notable features in this
balanced composition of sand,
water, and plants.

Ninna-ji is located in northwestern
Kyoto within the same hillside
district that includes Kinkaku-ji
and Ryoan-ji. Founded by Emperor
Kokaku in 886, construction was
completed by Emperor Uda only
after the founder's death. Ninna-ji
formerly served as the old Imperial
Palace of Omuro and was converted
to a temple upon Emperor Uda's
abdication and taking of the tonsure
at age thirty-five. The tradition of
the first or second son of an emperor
serving as head priest of the temple
continued for about one thousand
years, until the Meiji Restoration
of 1867.

There were at Ninna-ji originally
more than sixty sub-temples, but
the fifteenth-century Onin Wars
destroyed all the original structures. About a century later many
were reconstructed with funding
from both the Tokugawas and the
imperial household, and a number
of these buildings remain today.

About the turn of the twentieth
century yet another fire took its toll
on several of the buildings; these
have been rebuilt in the Momoyama
style and include the Shinden Hall
and a teahouse, the Mito-tei.

A horizontally trained pine tree
serves as the focal point of the
entry court inside the eastern gate;
the main garden lies beyond the
fence to the northeast of the Shinden
Hall. The original garden was supposedly designed in the Nanbokucho
style, a name derived from the
Nanboku period (c. 1336–1392)
when Japanese rule divided into two
rival imperial houses, often called
the northern and southern dynasties.
It is likely that the garden was heavily
modeled on the paradise gardens of
the Jodo sect with some influence,
perhaps, from the emerging Zen
faction. Shigemori Mirei credits
Shirai Dosho and Nyorai Do, who
modified the original scheme in
1690, as the real designers of the
garden seen today.

In the Zen tradition, the garden's
design includes vegetation as well
as areas of sand. Using the natural
slope of the site to advantage, the
garden was planned on two levels,
with the flat field of sand contrasted
against the inclined ground plane
blanketed with bushes and trees. A
waterfall dominates the entirety,
spilling into a pond that wraps
toward the east. Other features
include two teahouses and a stone
slab bridge from the Taisho period

● 仁和寺　右京区御室大内

91

that replaced an earlier earthen structure. Emperor Kokaku was particularly fond of the Hitotei (Flying Wave Arbor) which derived its name from the play of maple leaves upon the water when breezes drew their branches across the surface of the pond.

Note the variation in views and the appearances of various garden elements from differing positions along the veranda—a balanced composition of sand, water, and planting accompanies every shift in position. Also of interest is the acoustic effect of the splash of the waterfall upon rocks in the pond. Although originally designed to be walked through, the gardens can still be appreciated when viewed from the veranda of the Shinden. The Ninna-ji garden thus represents a transition from the *kaiyu* (stroll) to the *kansho* (admiration) style of garden in the late Edo period.

Comments: During mid to late April, an extremely fine grove of cherry trees near the temple's pagoda bloom to spectacular effect (not part of the garden).

Ninna-ji: View from the Shinden

Ryoan-ji　■

Ukyo-ku, Ryoan-ji,
Goryonoshita-cho

Muromachi period, 1499
Rinzai Zen Buddhism

Hours: 8:00 to 5:00 (March–
November); 8:30 to 4:30
(December–February)

Photography is permitted.

Special Features: An immaculate
composition of fifteen rocks surrounded by small areas of moss
and a large plane of raked gravel.
The wall enclosing the garden is
covered by a mottled patina of
lichen in brown hues and is itself
designated a national treasure.

The garden of Ryoan-ji (Dragon
Peace Temple) is the most famous
garden in Japan and certainly the
most photographed. The grounds
were originally the estate of a noble-
man of the powerful Fujiwara
family in the Heian period, but the
property later passed into the hands
of the Hosokawa family. The famous
general Hosokawa Katsumoto died
during the Onin Wars (1467–1477),
and according to his wishes the
estate became a temple of the Rinzai sect of Zen Buddhism under
the patronage of the nearby monastery, Myoshin-ji.

The buildings of the temple were
burned in the war but were rebuilt
near the end of the fifteenth century.

● 龍安寺　右京区龍安寺御陵下町

Ryoan-ji: The dry garden

The rock garden is believed to date from about 1500. The designer remains unknown, although Soami (1472–1523) often receives credit. A fire in 1790 ravished the temple, which was then reconstructed in its present form—the rock garden was apparently left undamaged by the blaze. Ryoan-ji is located somewhat outside Kyoto proper and remained relatively unknown until the 1930s. Praised by native and Western critics alike, the garden became widely celebrated in relatively short order.

Ryoan-ji is the supreme example of the dry (*kare-sansui*) garden in which rocks and raked gravel "symbolize" water or landscape elements. Except for moss around the base of the rocks, no plants grow within the walls. The fifteen stones form a masterful composition, skillfully arranged so that one rock remains hidden when seen from any point along the veranda. More abstract in its imagery than other Zen gardens, no effort tries to render idealized landscapes in more realistic materials (See also Daitoku-ji).

Many have tried to explain the meaning of the stones at Ryoan-ji; interpretations include "a mother tiger and her cubs swimming" to "islands in a sea"—but these titles are insignificant. Because these *kare-sansui* gardens were intended to support contemplation, their real meaning lay in the mind's realization of them through disciplined study. The visitor is still left to complete the landscape and, of course, its ultimate meaning. Many Zen priests contend that by intense meditation one may be transported into the garden, and that any scene, no matter what its actual size, may become infinite.

Like most Zen gardens, Ryoan-ji relies on a strong sense of enclosure for its mood. Partially for functional reasons, as the gardens were often a quiet escape during periods of civil turmoil in Kyoto, the surrounding wall also served as a visual boundary or ground against which the stones and gravel are positioned. Zen gardens such as Ryoan-ji also limited the viewing area to a designated and limited veranda. The prominent line of the tile roof both provided physical protection from the elements and demarcated a horizontal boundary overhead.

Comments: Ryoan-ji is a main stop on the tourist route and is often extremely crowded. At times recordings in Japanese tell the history of the garden, and how to enjoy it, from loudspeakers mounted in the rafters. But this garden can only be fully appreciated in solitude; go early in the morning or late in the afternoon.

1   2

3

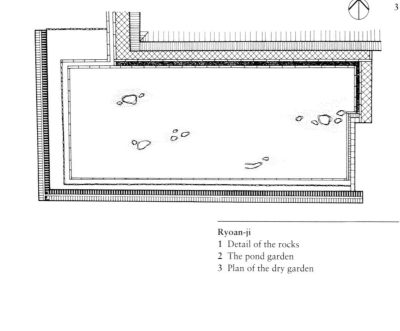

Ryoan-ji
1 Detail of the rocks
2 The pond garden
3 Plan of the dry garden

95

Kinkaku-ji (Rokuon-ji) The Golden Pavilion ■

Kita-ku, Kinkaku-ji-cho
Muromachi period, c. 1395
Shokoku-ji school of Rinzai
Zen Buddhism

Hours: 9:00 to 5:00

Photography is permitted.

Special Features: The Golden Pavilion (Kinkaku), a three-story viewing and pleasure pavilion with a brightly gilt exterior, is the focal point of the pond garden. The structure and garden are especially beautiful after a snowfall.

During the fourteenth century the influence of the Chinese Song dynasty swept over the Japanese arts, with Yoshimitsu, the third Ashikaga shogun (1358–1409), as its most elevated exponent. Gathering together artists, poets, and Zen priests returned from China, he built extravagantly, assuming the ideals of the Song period as well as those of the domestic Heian era. Yoshimitsu began construction of the Golden Pavilion shortly before he officially retired in 1394. While still maintaining political power, he passed the title to his nine-year-old son and moved to his new estate. Although few of Yoshimitsu's original buildings remain, we can experience remnants of the great estate in its sizable pond, rockwork, and extensive plantings.

The pavilion derives its architectural character from the Song style, its overall form recalling pavilions and buildings seen in paintings of the period. The pavilion took its name from Yoshimitsu's original plan to gild the ceiling of the third story. In 1950 a deranged student monk burnt down the unpainted pavilion, but an exact replica was built shortly thereafter—and it was decided that the structure should now literally match its name. Today the exterior of the pavilion glows with golden walls.

Yoshimitsu built the Kinkaku as the terminus of his sprawling palace complex following the precepts of the *shinden* style popular in the Heian period, and he positioned the structure on the edge of the pond to capture the most dramatic views. Some believe that the pavilion was once completely surrounded by water—like a fishing pavilion—with only an arched bridge connecting it to the main palace complex. The first story of the pavilion served as a reception room for guests and as a lakeside departure point for pleasure boating in ornate Chinese-style boats. The second story accommodated private discussions on art and the affairs of the day while offering a stunning panorama from its balcony. The third story served as a private refuge for Yoshimitsu and

---

Kinkaku-ji
1 The pavilion and pond
2 A view through the islands

1

2

close friends and accommodated contemplation and ceremonial tea drinking.

The grounds of the estate encompass four-and-a-half acres. Exquisitely pruned trees rim the large pond; Mt. Kinugasa rises beyond. By cleverly controlling the foreground, middle ground, and background of the garden the designers manipulated the garden spaces to increase their apparent size. Rocks and plantings of small scale dominate the foreground; beyond the island at the center of the pond, the plantings softly blend with the background, like the many peninsulas and coves of the undulating shoreline, extending the apparent boundaries of the garden. A widely used practice with early Chinese origins, the use of tightly composed landscape elements became more sophisticated in Japanese hands.

Yoshimitsu pursued architecture and gardens with remarkable vigor. In 1408 the emperor visited Kinkaku-ji: this is thought to be the first time an emperor resided with a person who was not a court noble. (The shogun, while military ruler of the nation, did not share imperial lineage.) This sojourn was an occasion of immense splendor and the culmination of Yoshimitsu's aesthetic career. He died shortly after the emperor's visit, and his glorious estate became a Zen temple, Rokuon-ji, as he had willed.

Koetsu-ji

Kita-ku, Takagamine, Koetsu-cho
Edo period, 1615
Nichiren Buddhism
Hours: 8:00 to 5:00
Photography is permitted.

The shogun Tokugawa Ieyasu granted the area that now comprises Koetsu-ji to Honami Koetsu (1557–1637) in 1615. Koetsu was a great tea master as well as a highly renowned and accomplished potter and calligrapher. Scion of sword makers and connoisseurs, Koetsu possessed great skill at metalworking and served both the nobility and warrior classes.

When Koetsu retired at the age of seventy-six, he moved to northern Kyoto, to the Taikyo-an, now called Koetsu-ji. Today there are several teahouses on these beautiful grounds that look out onto the Kyoto mountainside. The principal feature of the garden is a magnificently designed and crafted bamboo fence, attributed to Koetsu himself. Made of diagonally lashed bamboo, it curves gently around the periphery of one of the garden's teahouses. Koetsu-ji merits visiting if only to view this superb fence and teahouses and to enjoy the view and picturesque surroundings.

● 光悦寺　北区鷹峯光悦町

Koetsu-ji: The bamboo fence

Shoden-ji

Kita-ku, Nishigamo, Kitachinjuan-cho
Early Edo period
Nanzen-ji school of Rinzai
Zen Buddhism
Hours: 9:00 to 5:00
Photography is permitted.
Special Features: A dry garden
utilizing azaleas in place of the
usual rock groupings, and a
"borrowed scenery" view of
Mt. Hiei in the distance.

●
正伝寺　北区西賀茂北鎮守菴町

The often-overlooked temple of
Shoden-ji is situated in the uncrowded
northern end of Kyoto, a quiet
polished garden in heavily wooded
surroundings. The temple occupies
a hillside site at the end of a long
series of steps; the flattened shelf
upon which the buildings sit helps
engage the distant mountain range
above the tops of the neighboring
trees.

Shoden-ji's main garden lies east of
the Hojo (Superior's Quarters)
and is surrounded on two sides by
a tile-capped white clay wall. The
garden is unique in that groupings
of trimmed azaleas—rather
than the groups of rocks more
common to Zen garden designs—
grow from its white gravel base.
Shoden-ji is nonetheless a *kare-
sansui* (dry) garden in the classic
tradition: for example, the azaleas
are grouped in clusters of 7-5-3, like
the rocks in Zen gardens such as
Ryoan-ji.

The 7-5-3 (*shichi-go-san*) arrangement is a common ordering that
informed many of the Japanese arts.
Recommended in the Chinese *I-ching*,
the "harmony of odd numbers"
governed asymmetrical compositions
by employing only odd-numbered
groupings. Even-numbered groups
produced symmetrical compositions,
a manner generally avoided in early
Edo period gardens. The 7-5-3
configuration was also considered
particularly auspicious in terms of
health and longevity.

Viewing the garden from the
veranda, note that the clusters
increase in volume from right to
left, leading the eye to a gate in
the far wall. Dense planting of trees
border the garden on its right side;
with those on the corresponding
side of the garden they provide an
intensely contrasting dark-leafed
background to the white walls,
white gravel, and pink azaleas.
Beyond the wall, just above the tree
line, appears the silhouette of Mt.
Hiei, incorporated carefully into
the composition as yet another
effective example of "borrowed
scenery." In its passive appropriation,
however, this usage departs quite
significantly from that used at nearby
Entsu-ji, which also incorporates
Mt. Hiei as part of its design.

Comments: Shoden-ji is a pristine,
perfectly composed garden that
stands off the beaten track. As at
Entsu-ji, the "borrowed scenery"
is best experienced on a clear day.

1

2

Shoden-ji
1 View of the garden with Mt. Hiei beyond
2 Detail of dry garden with clipped shrubs

●

Southwest District
Kyoto Key Map

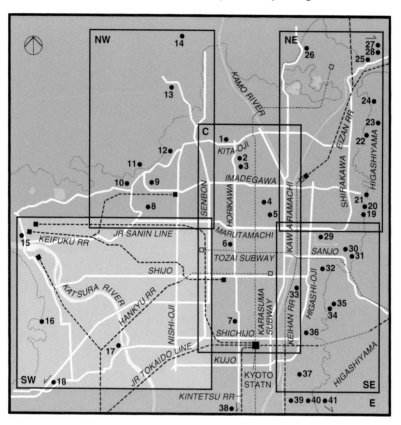

15 Tenryu-ji
16 Saiho-ji
17 Katsura Rikyu
18 Yoshimine-dera

Southwest District Map

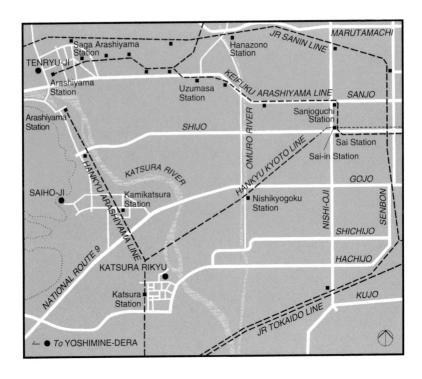

Tenryu-ji

Ukyo-ku, Saga, Tenryu-ji,
Susukinobaba-cho
Kamakura period, c. 1339
Headquarters of the Tenryu-ji
school of Rinzai Zen Buddhism
Hours: 8:30 to 5:30 (21 March–20
October); 8:30 to 5:00 (21 October–
20 March)
Photography is permitted.
Special Features: Grouping of seven
stones in the pond and the use of
"borrowed scenery."

Tenryu-ji was built by shogun
Ashikaga Takauji about 1339. The
priest Muso Kokushi, designer of
the moss garden at Saiho-ji and
regarded as one of Japan's great

garden designers and religious
figures, planned the garden.

The first construction on the site, the
villa of a prince, dates to the Heian
period; the estate then served as the
residence of Emperor Gosaga beginning in 1270. The exact form of the
villa and its gardens as they were
before Muso's intervention is unclear,
but in making the garden at Tenryu-ji
he created a Heian-style pond
garden that incorporated Chinese
aspects popular at the time. Although
the temple buildings have been
destroyed and rebuilt several times
(the present buildings date from the
Edo period), evidence of what must
have been a lavish landscape endures.

天龍寺　右京区嵯峨天龍寺芒ノ馬場町

Tenryu-ji

The principal feature of the garden is a grouping of seven rocks positioned near the shore at the rear of the pond. The strong vertical lines of the rocks thrusting from the water exemplify a Song dynasty style that contrasts with the more usual horizontal demeanor of Japanese rockwork. This beautiful arrangement appears precisely composed from any point in the garden, and attests to the skill of its designer. The reflection of the rocks in the water heightens their upright stance and adds tension to the composition without destroying its delicate balance.

Tenryu-ji represents a transitional style—a garden that hints at the contemplative landscapes of the later Muromachi period, while remaining firmly rooted in the court style of the Heian period.

Comments: Tenryu-ji was one of the first gardens, and the oldest still in existence, to use "borrowed scenery" (*shakkei*). Borrowed scenery incorporates distant landscape elements into the design. At Tenryu-ji, two mountains—Arashiyama and Kameyama—appear as part of the garden, appropriated and integrated into this splendid mix of water, rocks, and vegetation.

Tenryu-ji: The principal rock groupings

Saiho-ji (Kokedera) ∎
The Moss Temple

Nishikyo-ku, Matsuo, Jingatani-cho
Kamakura period, 1339
Rinzai Zen Buddhism
Hour: Permission from the temple
is required.
Photography is permitted.
Special Features: Over forty
varieties of moss blend into a
luxuriant texture that carpets the entire
garden. The maple trees display
excellent fall color.

Saiho-ji traces its origins to
the eighth century when the temple
was founded on its present site.
A major reconstruction took place
in 1339 under the direction of
the noted priest Muso Kokushi
(also known as Muso Soseki).
Muso was an avid garden builder
who believed firmly in the value of
meditating in the presence of gardens;
he wrote that the garden could be a
means by which to reach enlightenment. At Saiho-ji then, the garden
contributes a serene matrix in which
to contemplate the existence of
nature and the nature of existence.

●
西芳寺　西京区松尾神ヶ谷町

Saiho-ji: The moss carpet in winter

The temple complex originally comprised many buildings, with small residences and prayer halls dotting the hillside, but all of the structures were destroyed during the fifteenth-century civil wars. Today, the Founder's Hall, a more recent building, and two teahouses—one of which, the Shonan-tei, is thought to have been built in the Momoyama period—are classified as national treasures.

In the later part of the twelfth century considerable renovation had transformed the garden, and from this period Saiho-ji derived its form as a paradise garden. In Jodo (Pure Land) Buddhist belief the garden represented on earth the Western Paradise of the Amidha Buddha. Thus, Saiho-ji's pond and fulsome vegetation convey an image of Amidha's heavenly domain. While the Moss Temple has undergone several subsequent reconstructions, certain aspects of the Western Paradise garden endure.

The first impression when entering this sizable garden (approximately four-and-a-half acres) is that of a deeply forested place illuminated by a gleaming sheet of water. Moss covers every ground surface and even some of the vegetation. Shade, humidity, and the heavy moist clay soil have provided ideal conditions for this verdant blanket: Saiho-ji's most significant feature. In early summer, after the heavy rainfalls, the moss is everywhere a radiant green. Reflected in the water, its softening quality diffuses the contour of every surface. Lichens sheath the trunks of the tall coniferous trees, and abound on rocky areas that moss fails to cover. Although altered and reduced in size from its original state, the pond includes several islands joined by bridges and lined with stones tinted by time.

The mood of this remarkable garden is at times dark and primeval, at times shimmering and golden as the sunlight reflects on the surface of the water. One senses venerability at Saiho-ji, and at certain moments a solitary and curious enchantment pervades the garden in a manner like no other garden in Kyoto.

Moving through the garden and a bamboo grove, we pass through a gate, mount several steps, and enter an upper area known as the "dry cascade." This celebrated composition captures the essence of a mountain waterfall and is thought to be the first example in Japan of a dry landscape (*kare-sansui*). Here the rocks evince a pronounced horizontality that differs significantly from the Chinese-influenced vertical styles of the time (see Tenryu-ji). Carefully composed and positioned, its rocks are dappled with lichen and moss, blurring their edges and blending them into the hillside. It seems as if water will pour over their surfaces at any minute,

although it never will. The dry cascade at Saiho-ji is considered to have exerted a profound influence on many later gardens.

The changing seasons are dramatically set against the green background of this garden. In May, azaleas burst into a flaming scarlet. In July, large-leafed lotuses command the pond. In autumn, maple leaves glow crimson and orange-yellow. At one time there were cherry trees to harken spring, but alas, they no longer exist. Despite these moments of color, the greens dominate this world of moss and water.

Comments: The best time to enjoy the moss is usually from May to June, when the spring rains bring the garden to its height of beauty.

Until July 1977 Saiho-ji was open to the public. However, due to the enormous number of visitors—up to 8,000 per day—the abbot felt the garden was being irreparably damaged and closed it to the general public. Today, visitors first attend a talk (in Japanese) and copy part of a sutra, a practice that is at first troubling, but in time feels warranted. Permission to see the garden may be obtained by writing the temple. Hotels can normally aid in making reservations. Be sure to confirm the admission fee, however, for it is relatively expensive and continually increasing.

Saiho-ji: The pond

Katsura Rikyu
Katsura Imperial Villa

■

Nishikyo-ku, Katsura, Misono-cho
Edo period, 1620–1645

Hours: The villa is open on weekdays; Saturdays in April, May,
October, and November; and the
third Saturday of the other months.
It is closed on national holidays and
from 28 December to 4 January.
Tours last approximately one hour.
All visitors must secure advance
permission from the Kyoto office
of the Imperial Household Agency
located on the grounds of the Imperial
Palace (Gosho) in central Kyoto.
Tours start *promptly* and latecomers
are usually not admitted.

Photography is not permitted.

Special Features: The main building
of the villa, like its garden, is one
of the masterpieces of Japanese
environmental design. Remarkably
complex and beautiful arrangements of stepping stones are other
noteworthy features.

The Katsura Imperial Villa was the
creation and rural estate of Prince
Toshihito (1579–1629), the brother
of the Emperor Goyozei (1571–
1617). With Sento Gosho and
Shugaku-in, Katsura shares regard
as one of the high points of Japanese
garden art, and with them consti-
tutes the three imperial villas that
still grace Kyoto. The villa and
gardens were built over a period of
years, the prince's son, Toshitada
(1619–1662), adding to the villa
proper and making further refine-
ments to its grounds. The retired

emperor Gomizuno (1596–1680)
visited Katsura in 1658 while
work on his retreat Shugaku-in
progressed, and the Miyukiden (Hall
for Imperial Visits) was added
to the main building for this auspicious occasion. Within its elegant
wooden frame flawless and meticu-
lous detailing, rare woods, specially
created fastenings, and screen paintings combine with the finest craftsmanship to produce one of Japan's
unique architectural achievements.
In addition to the main villa, the
grounds also contain several rustic
teahouses and an extensive garden
focused on a central pond. The
garden layout, the rock and plant
compositions, and various other
elements—each is a treasure in itself.

Katsura, the earliest known stroll
garden, became the model and
garden ideal for subsequent noble
landscapes throughout the Edo period.
Stroll gardens, as the name implies,
invited the visitor to promenade
along a predetermined route. Gravel
or stepping stones paved the featured
path, with landscape elements
such as shrubs, hedges, and fences
modulating the pace, eye level, and
vistas opening to more distant parts
of the garden. Movement traced an
involved configuration designed so
that a body of water always stood
to the viewer's right.

The carefully planned stroll garden,
although novel for its time, borrowed
inspiration from the aesthetic of
tea. The stroll garden, like its tea

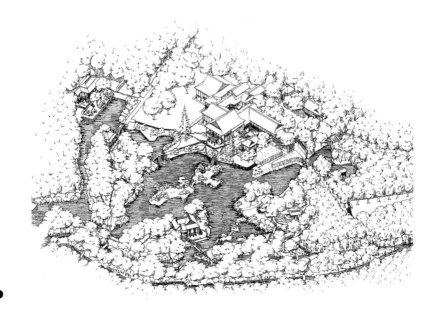

●

Katsura Rikyu: Axonometric drawing

garden predecessor, used sequential movement to reveal an almost limitless succession of views—like a grand drama whose scenes unfolded only through time. Unlike many of the earlier dry gardens, no one point provided a view over the entire landscape—one had to traverse its spaces to fully comprehend the garden's essence.

Many literary images incorporated into the garden's design enhanced the appreciation of its maker's intentions; a complete classical education allowed entry into its world of literary references as well. One garden scene might refer to a famous site in Japan; or to views described in classical, often Heian period, literature—bringing to mind passages and anecdotes familiar to well-read visitors. Prince Toshihito was an ardent admirer of the eleventh-century *Tale of Genji*, and the novel was said to have inspired many of the constructed vistas and literary allusions included in Katsura's design.

Moving through the grounds, the eye encountered constantly changing relationships of rustic teahouses, vegetation, lanterns, and lakeside views. Buildings appeared and disappeared, exposed in part or lost in greenery until the path finally approached the villa. Small spaces were made to seem larger by devices such as movement along an obliquely set path. Views also employed forced perspective; for example, the use of seemingly parallel hedges that actually converged to conjure an illusion of greater depth. Planned asymmetrically, the villa itself presented a mutable face when glimpsed from the garden route. And like the application of "hide and reveal" planning in the garden, the extensive use of sliding screens within the villa allowed a myriad of frames by which to view the landscape: various scenes defined and isolated in accord with personal desire or the particularities of the moment. By removing all the sliding panels the building opened completely to the garden, making possible an almost total merger of indoor and outdoor space.

The garden was long attributed to Japan's great landscape architect Kobori Enshu (1579–1647), but recent scholarship now suggests that Enshu participated little beyond consultation. The influence of Enshu, however, is most certainly felt at Katsura in the "Enshu style" that was such a dominant aesthetic force among the nobility during the early years of the seventeenth century. Both Prince Toshihito and his son were well schooled in the arts, and they directed the designing of Katsura with the help of skilled workmen and garden professionals, among them two of Enshu's brothers.

Katsura is especially noteworthy for its clever and subtle placement of stepping stones, which control movement as well as force views. The design of certain paths, for example, made walking in kimono and clogs quite difficult, coaxing visitors to look down to watch their steps. By lowering the eye to the ground, the designer cleverly prepared the visitor for a special prospect unveiled when he or she looked up. The planning of the walks also incorporated the use of *shin-gyo-so* (formal, semiformal, informal), a design principle utilized in many of the Japanese arts, although derived from the practice of calligraphy. Garden makers arranged their paths with varied formality—walking thus paralleled experiences in life. Many styles and juxtapositions of stones appear at Katsura, paired with the controlled use of plants to mask buildings or other parts of the garden. As one moves along these paths, these elements appear and disappear from view, always enticing the eye to the final destination: the three *shoin*. Only in time was the scene completed.

Numerous stone lanterns, each one of note, dotted the pathways and provided soft illumination at dusk and in the evenings. Stone and wooden bridges connected various areas of the garden, while the carefully composed rock groupings and specimen plantings, in restrained abundance, enriched the course of the journey.

In conclusion, Katsura was a garden for a nobility without political effect, a nobility with sufficient leisure to pursue the most elegant and comprehensive of the arts. In the garden, as if upon a theatre stage, hosts and guests acted out the controlled realities of everyday life as well as the illusions of life long past. Katsura and the stroll gardens that followed it were expressions of personal taste closely linked with an underlying aesthetic of courtly simplicity. True rivals for their intricate conception, careful design, resolution, and immaculate craftsmanship are very few.

Comments: Sited in the garden of Katsura is the rustic, yet especially beautiful teahouse, the Shokin-tei (Pine-lute Pavilion). The porch of the teahouse provides one of the best places from which to view the garden, for it affords outlooks across the pond in many directions. The pavilion itself is also one of the main subjects of view from several other points in the garden. Viewing and viewed were important concerns in Edo period design, and the garden exploited both conditions. The bamboo terrace before the villa, for example, was built especially for moon-viewing during August, an activity for which the Katsura district had long been noted.

Katsura Rikyu: Path and stepping stones

Katsura Rikyu
1 The Ama-no-hashidate peninsula
2 The *shoin*
3 Stepping stones overlay pebblework

1

2

3

Yoshimine-dera

Nishikyo-ku, Oharano,
Oshio-cho
Early Edo period
Tendai Buddhism
Hours: 8:00 to 5:00
Photography is permitted.
Special Features: A five-to-six-hun-
dred-year-old pine tree, unfortunately
reduced in dimension in recent years,
that has been trained to grow hori-
zontally.

This little-known temple is situated
in a somewhat rural setting to the
southwest of Kyoto, an area that
remains to this day the least popu-
lated district. Yet it retains much
of its centuries-old character. To
reach the temple one travels a road
through abundant bamboo forests
harvested for their edible shoots and
for stalks used for a myriad of deco-
rative and architectural purposes.

Sited on the mountainside, the
temple is approached by a long
series of paths and steps. Its
structures occupy several levels
carved from the steep hillsides. On
all levels gardens display many out-
standing mature plant specimens,
the salient features of the complex.
The finely sheared azaleas, cherries,
and maples also demonstrate considerable horticultural skill and contribute to the beauty of the whole.

The truly notable feature of
Yoshimine-dera is a Japanese white
pine tree (*Pinus pentaphylla*)—known

to be between five and six hundred
years old—that grows along two
sides of the temple's upper level.
From a central trunk, the branches
have been trained to grow horizontally at right angles to one another,
about five feet off the ground, in a
spreading effect said to resemble
"opening arms." At one time not
too long ago each side measured
over seventy feet (twenty meters)
long, with a total length of over one
hundred eighty-five feet (fifty-four
meters). Unfortunately, the effects
of old age and the pine weevil
necessitated pruning a considerable
section of the tree; although still
impressive in aspect, today it displays less of its prior glory. The
approach by stairs to this area once
emerged directly beneath the tree,
adding to the dramatic effect. Even
in its reduced state, the tree snaking
along the edge of the plateau well
represents its name, "Gliding
Dragon Pine" (*Yuryumatsu*). A
trip to the temple just to see this
original work of living art is easily
justified.

Comments: There are several other
lesser-known, but equally interesting, temples near Yoshimine-dera,
such as Komyo-ji and Shoji-ji.
One can easily spend a day walking
through the bamboo groves,
visiting temples and villages, and
enjoying the alluring surroundings.

● 善峯寺 西京区大原野小塩町

1

2

Yoshimine-dera
1 Upper level with pine
2 The Gliding Dragon Pine

119

Northeast District
Kyoto Key Map

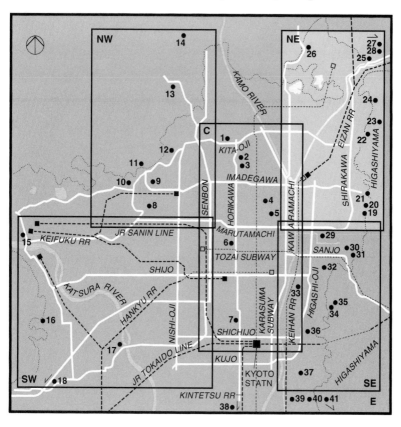

19 Anraku-ji
20 Honen-in
21 Ginkaku-ji
22 Shisen-do
23 Manshu-in
24 Shugaku-in
25 Renge-ji
26 Entsu-ji
27 Sanzen-in
28 Jakko-in

Northeast District Map

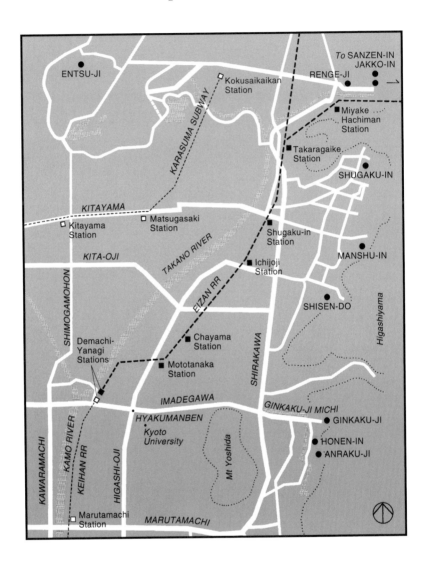

Anraku-ji

Sakyo-ku, Shishigatani, Goshonodan-cho

Kamakura period, founded c. 1212; Hondo c. 1581

Nishiyamazenrinji school of Jodo Buddhism

Hours: Not normally open to the public; permission for entry must be secured from the temple.

Photography is permitted.

Special Features: Tightly clipped azaleas that bloom profusely in spring.

The modest temple of Anraku-ji is associated with Honen (1133–1212), the founder of Jodo Buddhism (see Honen-in), and Anraku (?–1207), one of his disciples. The ex-emperor Gotoba (1179–1239) ordered the death of Anraku after he and the priest Juren had converted two of the emperor's favorite court ladies to the sect. Conspirators from the Jodo sect rumored that Anraku's and Juren's intentions were less than honorable, enraging Gotoba and leading him to take these extreme measures against the priests and cult.

The temple is located close to Honen-in in the quiet neighborhood of Shishigatani. Upon entering the grounds through an unpretentious gate, one sees the low hedge that lines the stone path leading to the Main Hall (Hondo). The building rises above the pruned shrubs and hedges that surround it, their rounded forms mirroring the wooded Higashiyama hills that backdrop the temple grounds. In addition to the Hondo, a *shoin* building features gardens on both its east and west sides.

As with many other Kyoto temples, the architecture of corridors and buildings at Anraku-ji enclose a number of gardens. When the sliding screens of the temple structures open in any number of differing combinations, an intensified view of one garden after another results, creating a great sense of depth and added visual interest.

Various restorations have left their marks on the Anraku-ji gardens and today they contain particularly fine specimens of azaleas and camellias. Moss also exerts a vigorous presence as a verdant groundcover, and clipped azaleas flank the handsome stone path at the temple's front gate. Weighty and sculptural, they bloom freely and present a showy splash of bright color (in many gardens selective picking of blossoms limits the impact of the flowers and helps to confine attention to the volumes of the shrubs). When compared to the subdued color of most Kyoto gardens, the azaleas of springtime Anraku-ji tend to overwhelm. Anraku-ji might fittingly be called the "azalea temple," and is opened to the public only during the time of this display.

●

安楽寺　左京区鹿ヶ谷御所ノ段町

123

Honen-in

Sakyo-ku, Shishigatani,
Goshonodan-cho
Early Edo period
Jodo Buddhism
Hours: 9:00 to 4:00
Photography is permitted.
Special Features: Two rectangular
sand mounds with raked designs.
Good fall color.

Honen-in is named after Honen
(1133–1212), who founded the Jodo
sect of Buddhism in the beginning
of the thirteenth century and
erected a statue of Amidha on
the present site. The main halls and
gardens date from the middle of
the seventeenth century when Jodo
came under the patronage of the
Tokugawas. Some rooms from
Toyotomi Hideyoshi's Fushimi
Momoyama Castle were transferred
here in the seventeenth century,
augmenting the existing buildings:
these famous apartments, originally
built in the closing years of the prior
century, were reconstructed to open
upon their own private garden.

The history of Jodo Buddhism is
marked by centuries of hardship
and persecution. In its infancy, the
sect struggled against the older,
more established, denominations
that tried to destroy it. Faithful
believers persevered, however, and
eventually the sect began to flourish
through Tokugawa intervention.
Today, Jodo Buddhism is the second largest sect in Japan, surpassed
only by the Shin sect which is
considered an offshoot of Jodo.

Honen-in occupies a thickly
wooded slope of Higashiyama,
about a ten-minute walk south of
the Silver Pavilion (Ginkaku-ji).
Entry to the temple precinct follows
a series of wide stone steps that lead
to a wooden gateway. Turning left
immediately, a series of rising steps
leads obliquely to the main walk.
Maple trees planted in a plush bed
of moss contribute to the effect of
this exquisitely detailed gravel walkway. As the culmination of the
path, rough-hewn stone steps lead
to a second gate—this with a thatch
roof—set at a slight angle to the
footpath. The approach and entry
sequence have turned and elevated
the visitor through the judicious
placement of steps and walks.
Ahead lies the gate and threshold
of the garden.

Once inside the gate, the eye falls
immediately on two large sand
mounds bracketing the path. Every
few weeks, priests renew or modify
the designs raked into the tops of
the mounds. At times the designs
reflect the seasons, using such
motifs as the maple leaf for autumn;
nonseasonal references also contribute designs, such as an abstraction of water. Beyond the mounds,
two buildings stand—a storehouse
to the left and a bathhouse to the
right. A stone bridge crosses a small
pond that fronts the main hall.

● 法然院　左京区鹿ヶ谷御所ノ段町

1

2

Honen-in
1 View of garden with sand mounds
2 Raked sand design

125

A linear pathway composed of rough-cut stones encircles the main hall, offering a new view with each turn. To the rear, a small pond garden faces the Fushimi apartments, but it is not normally open to the public.

Honen-in is an amalgam of many garden elements, an additive composition of sand mounds, pond, and walks, all expertly laid out and integrated for a tasteful effect. Add to this formation the temple's collection of plant types, particularly the maples with their dazzling fall colors, and another of Kyoto's unique gardens emerges.

Comments: The wooded area surrounding Honen-in is quiet and pleasurable, a tranquil alternative to the busy streets of Kyoto. Unlike nearby Ginkaku-ji, crowds rarely plague Honen-in. Just to the west runs the Shirakawa river that parallels the string of temples along the Higashiyama. The banks of the river have been planted with cherry trees and are now christened the "Philosopher's Walk." Strolling the paths along the river and visiting Higashiyama's many temples makes for an especially enjoyable day.

Honen-in: Raked sand design

Ginkaku-ji (Jisho-ji)   ■
The Silver Pavilion

Sakyo-ku, Ginkaku-ji-cho
Muromachi period, c. 1480
Shokoku-ji school of Rinzai
Zen Buddhism

Hours: 8:30 to 5:00 (15 March–
30 November); 9:00 to 4:30
(1 December–14 March)

Photography is permitted.

Special Features: The Silver
Pavilion (Ginkaku), a two-story
pleasure pavilion, now designated
a national treasure. An unusual
garden combining both sand and
pond areas. Good fall color.

The buildings of the Ginkaku-ji
temple complex originally constituted
the retirement villa of the shogun
Ashikaga Yoshimasa (1435–1490),
but upon his death the complex was
converted to the Zen temple of
Jisho-ji. The Togu-do Hall at the
temple contains a room thought by
many to be the prototype of the teahouse. Yoshimasa was the grandson
of Shogun Ashikaga Yoshimitsu,
the builder of the Golden Pavilion
(see Kinkaku-ji). In pursuit of artistic
originality and in homage to his
grandfather, Yoshimasa intended
to cover portions of the two-story
wooden pavilion with silver leaf.
Although this dream never materialized, the idea captured the imagination of the Japanese people, and the
name "Silver Pavilion" has endured.

The pavilion overlooks a conceptually complex garden, at times
attributed to Soami, consisting of
two contrasting sections carefully
composed and balanced in delicate
equilibrium. The first, the pond area
adjacent to the pavilion, features
compositions of rocks and plants
designed to be seen from multiple
viewpoints. Picturesque landscape
scenes inspired by Japanese and
Chinese literature infuse this part of
the garden. Its features and vistas
often allude to, and are named for,
celebrated places in literature, which
adds to the considerable enjoyment
of the well-read garden visitor.

In contrast to the vegetal inclusion
that characterizes the pond garden
stand two sculptured mounds of sand
that counterpoise the pavilion standing nearby. The strong form of the
truncated cone—The Moon-Viewing
Height—suggests images such as
Mt. Fuji or the central mountain of
Buddhism. The lower horizontal
mound—The Sea of Silver Sand—
is so named for its appearance by
moonlight. Both sand banks were a
later, Edo period addition to the
garden. Sand used to replenish garden paths was kept in storage heaps,
and in time Zen priests came to
regard their aesthetic potential for
transforming the existing garden.

The juxtaposition of dry and pond
garden elements at Ginkaku-ji
departs from common practice.
Though some experts find a certain
clumsiness of design and inappro-
priateness in feeling due to the forms
and material of the mounds, the
authors do not share this view.

● 銀閣寺　左京区銀閣寺町

1

2

3

It is just this contrast, in fact, that generates so much of the garden's aesthetic power. The garden of the Silver Pavilion remains unique in Japanese garden history because of this rare combination of vocabularies and the skill with which they were shaped and juxtaposed. In a sweeping assumption so common to Zen, contrasts are not distinguished as opposites but as parts of the same whole.

A carefully modeled progression of spaces leads from the street to the temple, forging a sophisticated transition from the outside world to the world of the garden. A tree-lined approach marks the temple entrance, a roofed gateway standing at its end. As we pass through this first gate, a hedge blocks our movement and directs us to the right. Confined by stone walls and high, immaculately clipped hedges, we turn and follow the formal walkway, which terminates in yet another hedge. The path turns once again, this time to the left. Passing through a second gate into a less formal court, we glimpse the sand area of the garden through a bell-shaped opening in the far wall—a preview of what will follow.

By a series of stages—the most formal and geometrically structured marking the entrance—the progression of movement eases the passage from the chaos and pressures of the everyday into the tranquility and ultimate reality of the garden universe. (See Daitoku-ji for a related spatial progression.)

Ginkaku-ji
1 The entry corridor
2 The entry garden
3 The Silver Pavilion
4 The Sea of Silver Sand
5 The pond and Togu-do

129

4

5

Shisen-do ▪

Sakyo-ku, Ichijo-ji,
Monguchi-cho
Edo period, 1636
Hours: 9:00 to 5:00 (last entry 4:40)
Photography is permitted.
Special Features: A jewel of garden
design, intimate in scale yet vast
in implication.

The face that Shisen-do presents to
the street does little to suggest the
realm of tranquility and engagement
found within its walls: a small
rustic gate, a few stepping stones in
the sand, a simple bamboo fence.
The scale is intimate and enclosed.

Light from an opening in the
pavilion at the entry draws the
visitor inward, with a suggestion of
rewards to come. Looking beyond
the veranda the visitor enjoys a beautiful view of the raked sand, sheared
azalea forms, and the tree-covered
hillside of Higashiyama. The garden
feels equipoised yet fragile—in delicate balance with the forces of nature
and the topographical setting.

Although the Edo period saw little
actual warfare, the period was
hardly quiet. A rising anti-Tokugawa
sentiment developed, expressing
itself in a number of seemingly
unrelated ways, among them
garden design. Ishikawa Jozan
(1583–1672), exiled by Tokugawa
Ieyasu for opposing certain aspects
of the latter's military rule, escaped
to Kyoto where he studied tea, the
arts, philosophy, and garden design.

In 1636 he built Shisen-do, so named
for the portraits of thirty-six
Japanese and Chinese poets that
line the wall of one of the buildings.
Here he lived for forty years until
his death in 1672.

Ishikawa was a learned and sensitive man. His garden ideas turned
from the rigid interpretation of tradition more typical of the period and
the dicta that governed the tea garden, instead formulating a design in
the "scholar's style." Elements of both
the historical dry garden and nascent
stroll garden appeared at Shinsen-do,
where intimacy and personal taste
prevailed over ostentatious display.

Shisen-do: Entry court

詩仙堂　左京区一乗寺門口町

131

The existing garden probably resembles its form in Jozan's time only in part; certainly the lower garden areas are relatively recent additions.

As viewed from the veranda, the careful composition of *karikomi*, or clipped shrubs, forms the garden's principal subject. The watchful eye and shears of the gardener keeps the form of the azaleas in constant perfection. But azaleas change in texture and color throughout the year and burst into a vivid pink in the spring. In the Japanese manner, many of the blossoms are selectively plucked to mute this brilliance, but even limited color effectively changes the space of the garden by restraining the eye in the foreground.

Shisen-do also uses the vegetation of the adjacent hillside as part of its design. Beyond the close forms of the azaleas and raked sand, the rear of the garden carefully blends with the trees of the surroundings, incorporating them into the overall composition. The softness of the many greens, the brilliance of the maples in their fall color, and the pinks of the azaleas in spring make Shisen-do a beautiful garden at any time of the year.

Of notable interest is the relationship of indoor and outdoor spaces at Shisen-do and the manner by which they are defined. From the *tatami*-covered floor of the interior, across the brilliant red cloth and rich brown of the venerable wooden veranda planks, space flows fluidly between inside and out. The contrast of the interior darkness with the brilliant light of the garden beyond is strong yet not harsh. As an intermediary zone, the veranda renders a transition in both light level and spatial constriction. Just where inside ends and outside space begins is difficult to establish with precision.

In the lower garden a stream feeds a small pond. A bamboo device called a "water clacker" collects water from the stream, dips to discharge its liquid cargo after filling, and then rapidly rises, with one end striking a carefully positioned stone with a sharp cracking sound. Once used to frighten deer, today it contributes only an aural comment on the passing of time. Although the lower gardens display some interest and charm in themselves, they cannot rival the magnificent upper garden and hillside surveyed from the veranda.

1

2

3

Shisen-do:
1 Detail of clipped azaleas in bloom
2 View from veranda
3 The lower garden area

Manshu-in

Sakyo-ku, Ichijo-ji,
Takenouchi-cho
Early Edo period
Tendai Buddhism
Hours: 9:00 to 5:00
Photography is permitted.

Manshu-in stands at the foot of the
Higashiyama hills in northeast Kyoto,
between the temple of Shisen-do and
the imperial villa of Shugaku-in.
The temple was first built by Saicho,
the founder of Tendai Buddhism
and its main temple Enryaku-ji on
Mt. Hiei. Originally located on the
mountain, Manshu-in was transferred to its present site about 1656.

The main garden includes an expanse
of sand that supports an island
and several miniature promontories
of moss featuring restrained
planting and arrangements of
stone. On one of these peninsulas,
sand runs beneath a bridge in a
convincing waterfall composition.
Also present are skillful repre-
sentations of the crane and tortoise
themes, executed with groupings
of stones and shrubs (see Konchi-in
at Nanzen-ji for a description of
the crane and tortoise theme). A
specimen pine tree positioned on
the central island showcases one of
its horizontal branches allowed to
achieve considerable length. Beyond
the garden's limits, a forested area
extends up the hillside and forms
a green background to the design.

The lack of a strict rectangular
enclosure distinguishes the garden
at Manshu-in, creating an especially
relaxed physical setting. The pre-
dominance of soft curving lines
graces the garden with a feeling
of flow that avoids any sense of
unresolved motion.

Manshu-in: View of the dry garden

● 曼殊院　左京区一乗寺竹ノ内町

Shugaku-in Rikyu
Shugaku-in Imperial Villa ■

Sakyo-ku, Shugaku-in
Edo period, 1659

Hours: The villa is open on weekdays; Saturdays in April, May,
October, and November; and the
third Saturday of the other months.
It is closed on national holidays and
from 28 December to 4 January.
Tours last about an hour. The guides
speak only Japanese. All visitors
must secure advance permission
from the Kyoto office of the Imperial
Household Agency located on the
grounds of the Old Imperial Palace
(Gosho). Allow several days after
applying to receive permission to
enter. Be prompt: tours start on time.

Photography is permitted.

Special Features: A magnificent
panoramic view of "borrowed
scenery" from the upper garden,
and an immense clipped hedge
(*karikomi*) screening the western
bank of the upper pond.

Shugaku-in Rikyu was the retreat
of the Emperor Gomizuno (1596–
1680) and is one of three imperial
villas to enhance Kyoto with their
beautiful gardens (see also Katsura
and Sento Gosho). Built as a private
retreat after the emperor's abdication
in 1629, it was funded with resources
provided by the Tokugawa shoguns.
Gomizuno constructed the magnificent estate at the base of Kyoto's
heavily wooded northeastern mountains on the site of a former temple.
Shugaku-in was never considered
an official residence; the emperor

regarded the villa as a place of
recreation and aesthetic pursuits.
Relatively light in construction and
ultimately fragile, the residential
structures and pavilions accommodated stays of only short duration.
These delicate structures blended
into the landscape and were graced
by a sense of being a part of the
natural environment.

The emperor visited Shugaku-in
several times a year, and records
reveal that he stayed at the villa
over seventy times during his life-
time. Since a grand entourage was
de rigeur, these excursions created
numerous problems of logistics and
protocol consonant with the retired
emperor's exalted position.

Gomizuno was a man of elevated
taste and artistic skills, who also
possessed a strong and sensitive
personality. While emperor, he
often contended with the military
rulers, and not until after his abdication was he treated more kindly
by the shogunate. After he renounced
his official duties, the Tokugawas
encouraged him to build a villa.
The prolonged search for a site in
the northern area of the city ended
in a suitable locale near Shugaku-in
village, and construction began
in the 1650s. It is thought that
the emperor designed the gardens
himself—in the manner of Kobori
Enshu—in collaboration with skilled
artisans and designers. Enshu,
deceased by this time, undoubtedly
still exerted a strong influence on

● 修学院離宮

左京区修学院

135

Gomizuno due to their earlier consultations regarding the grounds of the Sento Gosho. The combination of Enshu's influence and the retired emperor's familiarity with other famous gardens in Kyoto—the Katsura Villa, for example—inspired the creation of one of Japan's masterpieces of landscape art.

In extent, Shugaku-in comprises three separate villas with their gardens, sited at various elevations on a hillside of terraced rice fields. The gardens are now connected by tree-lined gravel paths added in 1890 to replace the former narrow trails.

1

The Lower Villa

Having entered the grounds of Shugaku-in, visitors pass through several gates to arrive at the lower garden beyond the Miyuki-mon (Imperial Gate). Here we note that this part of the villa conceptually centers on a structure known as the Jugetsu-kan, a restoration of Gomizuno's original dating from 1824. Vegetation inundates this structure. The front garden contains a finely contrived stream that empties into a pond below the villa. An area of sand, with gracefully positioned stepping stones, greets the adjacent veranda of the Jugetsu-kan. Also present are three stone lanterns of note, the most famous set adjacent to the path and known as the "Sleeve-shaped Lantern" (that is, kimono sleeve), or alternatively, the "Alligator's Mouth." It does indeed bear a passing resemblance to both these references. The garden of the lower villa is not large; the surrounding trees create a sense of enclosure. Like all of the gardens at Shugaku-in, maintenance is exquisite.

Shugaku-in
1 The hedge-covered dam
2 The Chitose Bridge in the upper garden

The Middle Villa

After leaving the lower villa, guests follow the gravel path south about two hundred meters and reach the middle villa, built as a residence for Gomizuno's eighth daughter, Princess Ake. This complex originally consisted of only the elegantly refined Rakushi-ken and its pond garden, but an elegantly embellished reception hall moved in 1682 from the princess' former palace augmented the original construction. Set on a higher level, this pavilion affords an ornate counterpoint to the more simple Rakushi-ken. When the princess became a nun in 1680, the temple structures now known as Rinkyu-ji were erected nearby.

The pond garden section of this grouping has continued in splendid condition to this day, although some of the structures were subsequently removed from the west side of the Rakushi-ken to make room for a lawn containing a notable pine tree trained to spread horizontally and fittingly termed an "umbrella pine" (*kasamatsu*). Also worth mention is a stone lantern said to contain Christian symbols made at a time when the foreign religion was proscribed. The carved image at the base is said to represent Mary, and two lines cut on the pedestal are reputed to depict the separated lines of the cross.

2

The Upper Villa

To reach the upper villa, guests return to the main route and continue to a point where the path branches in two directions. The path to the right, lined with pine trees, turns sharply uphill toward the villa above. A glance to the left, over the rice fields, reveals an immense, multitiered hedge which conceals the western embankment that dams the pond of the upper garden. This stunning vegetal mass comprises some forty varieties of shrubs, allowing only an occasional tree to break the horizontal lines of its sheared forms. The stepping of the hedge/dam form recalls, at least metaphorically, the terracing of the surrounding rice fields with their tiered paddies. A truly powerful form, it cannot fail to impress the visitor with its unique configuration and clever disguise of what might otherwise have been a rather awkward condition. The path continues upward, arriving at the Imperial Gate that controls entry to the most spectacular garden at Shugaku-in.

As one enters the gate under a dark canopy of trees, the path immediately veers right and mounts a narrow flight of stone steps constrained on both sides by a high hedge. After climbing through this constricted passage, one emerges into the sunlight at a high point beneath the Rinun-tei (Pavilion in the Clouds). Turning, looking northwest, guests encounter an incredible landscape panorama. Suddenly revealed is "borrowed scenery" (*shakkei*) on the grandest scale: the distant hills skillfully enter the garden in one of the most inspired examples of this Japanese design technique. The impact of the view is compounded by the contrast between the dark, enclosed approach, the explosion into light, and the grand vista that follows. Thus, one experiences how sequence heightens the garden's ultimate effect.

The upper villa garden centers on a large pond about two-and-a-half acres in size, known as Yokuryu-chi (Bathing Dragon Pond). This name is thought to derive from the shape of stones that jutted from the islands in the garden's early days, before its many plants had blanketed them into near invisibility. The pond is formed by the earthen dam to the west mentioned above, now covered by vegetation shaped by shears. Pleasure boating was a favorite activity on the pond; its layout of islands, coves, islets, and peninsulas all contributed to the pleasure of the excursion. Bridges and paths link the various islands to each other and to the shore, assuring a smooth passage through the wondrous landscape.

Walking along the eastern shore of the pond, guests passed the wooden Chitose-bashi (Bridge of Eternity) and the Kyusui-tei pavilion. The scenery and views along the pathway change continually, with

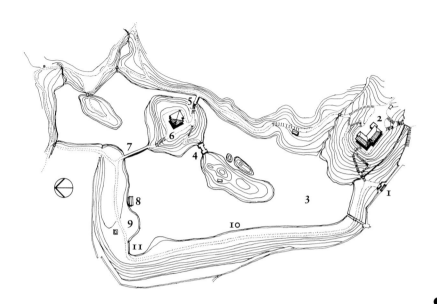

1 Imperial Gate
2 Rinun-tei
3 Pond
4 Chitose Bridge
5 Maple Bridge
6 Kyusui-tei
7 Earthen Bridge
8 Boathouse
9 Site of Shishisai
10 West Bank
11 Boat Landing

islands and corridors of foliage emerging or vanishing from sight. A bridge or other structures in the distance appears and then disappears from view, enticing the eye onward to more beautiful scenes. To the west, trees and foliage along the embankment create a matchless sight, especially when silhouetted against the skies at sunset.

At the north edge of the pond a boathouse near the former summer-house Shishisai enters view. From this point, looking back southward across the garden, the Rinun-tei can be seen perched above the lake, nestled into its fine vantage point. Note also the manner by which the

garden, with its formally sheared foliage, rises from the water and then softly blends into the forest, the vegetation becoming more natural in form as it ascends the mountain-side. This pruning technique, which tries to merge the garden with its surroundings, lengthens the vista and thereby seems to enlarge the garden.

Along the west side of the pond, one witnesses over the hedge a fine view of Kyoto in the distance. This path, added in an 1800s restoration, leads back to the point of entry. Some historians believe that visitors originally entered the garden through the Imperial Gate, boarded a boat at the edge of the pond, and sailed to

Shugaku-in: View westward over the dam

the Shishisai for a short rest or tea. From this point they might first enjoy boating and then proceed to the Rinun-tei along the eastern shore. If this was in fact the prescribed progression, the location of the path would be in keeping with the traditional stroll garden practice of keeping the water always to the stroller's right (see Katsura Villa). And since the passage would thus utilize a circuitous route to the Rinun-tei from the north, the surprise of the borrowed scenery would not have been lost.

Comments: The garden at Shugaku-in is a tribute to Gomizuno's talents and originality. Not only does Shugaku-in offer the visitor a truly great stroll garden, but also the use of borrowed scenery on an unparalleled scale. It is a thoroughly original design and marks a high point in Japan's garden history. Though the emperor did not exercise true political power at the time, he could at least create the illusion that he possessed virtually all the landscape. The garden borrowed the distant landscape to such a degree that no one has ever matched the scope of Gomizuno and company's accomplishments at Shugaku-in. One might easily imagine the emperor sitting in his pavilion at sunset, reading from *The Tale of Genji* or composing poetry, glancing up occasionally to view the maples in full color, while surveying the heavenly beauty of the world he had created—with the help of countless workmen, to be sure.

Renge-ji

Sakyo-ku, Kamitakano,
Hachiman-cho
Early Edo period
Tendai Buddhism
Hours: 9:00 to 5:00
Photography is permitted.
Special Features: Renge-ji lanterns;
fall color

蓮華寺　左京区上高野八幡町

The diminutive, yet poetic garden
of Renge-ji lies just off the beaten
path in northeast Kyoto. An unassuming gate marks the entrance,
from which a formal stone walkway
leads directly to the *shoin;* to the
right, a similar walk turns at a right
angle through a *torii* (gate) and
approaches the Hondo (Main Hall).
A large ginkgo tree, whose golden
leaves dazzle the eye in autumn,
shades this entry area.

Approaching the shoin, one encounters a gate to the right, and although
a horizontal bamboo rod bars entry,
the open gate affords an enticing
view into the pleasant garden
beyond. This same garden is also
viewed from the veranda of the shoin.

The garden's central area includes
a pond filled by water flowing from
the northern mountains with a
backdrop provided by plantings on
the north shore and the hillside
beyond. The stones, bridge, and
plantings double in their reflections
on the water's surface, in effect
enlarging the calm provided by the
small-scale foliage. The water's edge

is a masterfully treated combination
of rocks, tightly shaped shrubs, and
moss, all of which unite in a unique
fabric. Of note is a "turtle" rock
with an azalea growing from it,
which can be seen in the pond.

The lantern atop one of the shoreline rocks represents the Renge-ji
style and is characterized by a steep,
rounded cap. Stone lanterns, at first
used for only functional reasons
in the tea garden, increased in popularity during the Edo period, a
fashion that continues to the present
day. While the lanterns currently in
the garden are only replicas, they
differ only slightly in detail from the
originals.

The garden of Renge-ji, while a
conglomerate of styles, continues
to encourage multiple visits. The
lush green walls of foliage, reflected
and layered, conjure a serene and
beautiful setting. The perfected
detail, one of its principal strengths,
and excellent maintenance set the
stage for a quiet, idyllic experience.

Comments: Renge-ji is superb in
the fall when the maples and
ginkgo display their brilliant color.

142

1

2

Renge-ji
1 View of the garden across the pond
2 Shoreline rockwork

143

Entsu-ji

Sakyo-ku, Iwakura, Hataeda-cho
Early Edo period
Myoshin-ji school of Rinzai
Zen Buddhism
Hours: 10:00 to 4:00
Photography by permission.
Special Features: "Borrowed
scenery" view incorporating the
distant Mt. Hiei into the garden.

Located in the village of Hataeda,
just north of Kyoto proper, Entsu-
ji occupies the site of a former villa
of Emperor Gomizuno, which
originally contained several buildings disposed on different hillside
levels. But after the Shugaku-in
Rikyu was completed in 1659, the
Hataeda villa no longer served for
imperial visits. In 1678 the buildings
became the temple of Entsu-ji, although
the original complex was far larger
than the buildings existing today.

The small garden of Entsu-ji
features a composition of moss
combined with low clumps of plants
and stones. Deeply set into the
ground and horizontal in orientation,
the groupings appear to be natural
rock outcroppings. A low hedge
borders the garden on three sides,
crisply defining the garden's limits.
Beyond the hedge, a luxuriant
bamboo grove to one side counters
a tightly pruned living wall. To the
east is a stand of cryptomeria and
cypress trees, several of which rise
within the hedge and effectively
define the temple's garden. The

foliage line of the trees has been
purposefully trimmed up quite high,
framing a view of Mt. Hiei in the
distance.

Entsu-ji thus illustrates a more
intimate form of "borrowed
scenery" masterfully handled.
An impressive view alone does not
create borrowed scenery. Some
exacting middle-ground device
must bind the near garden with the
distant scenery to integrate the
borrowed elements as a natural part
or extension of the garden. The
manicured foreground elements and
boundary hedge yield to the middle-
ground foliage of the bamboo and
trees which function as a template
that directs the view through the
trunks and branches to the mountain beyond. The vertical lines of
the trunks intensify the sense of
depth and by their careful placement pull the mountain into the
garden.

There have been manifold variations
on the theme of borrowed scenery,
and several examples enrich the
gardens of today's Kyoto (see also
Joju-in, Shugaku-in, and Shoden-ji).
Appropriating scenery through a
field of trees is one of the more
common techniques; it parallels the
layering of space used in woodblock prints. Entsu-ji is among the
finest examples of this type.

There has been considerable specu-
lation that Emperor Gomizuno
was inspired by Entsu-ji when he
incorporated a borrowed scene

● 円通寺　左京区岩倉幡枝町

into his gardens at Shugaku-in. But there is a fundamental difference in the use of appropriation at Shugaku-in, which is a stroll garden, and Entsu-ji, where the scene is viewed from a static vantage point. Movement in this garden would destroy the delicate scale relationships created by the particular placement of particular features.

Comments: It is best to visit Entsu-ji on a clear day: just after a rain, on a breezy day, or even a sharp wintry morning. Kyoto is often hazy or smoggy and in the summer the sky is a washed-out white, particularly at midday. The haze obscures the distant mountain or at least make it appear quite faint. On the other hand, the effect on a misty day can be very beautiful: although the view of Mt. Hiei may be lost, the softness can exaggerate the sense of depth. It should be obvious, however, that the technique works best when Mt. Hiei stands out distinctly as an integral part of the garden. One can only hope that the city's environmental conditions will continue to improve in time, adding to the health and enjoyment of natives and visitors alike, today and tomorrow.

Entsu-ji: The borrowed view

Sanzen-in

Sakyo-ku, Ohara, Raikoin-cho
Heian period, founded c. 985;
additional structures and the
gardens date from the Edo period.

Tendai Buddhism

Hours: 8:30 to 4:30 (March–
November); 8:30 to 4:00
(December–February)

Photography is permitted but
no tripods.

Special Features: The Main Hall of
this temple complex sits in a simple
garden alive with brilliant maple
trees in the fall.

Sanzen-in is located in the extreme
north of Kyoto in the rural village
of Ohara. In its early days, the
temple was considered remote, for
Ohara was the last village in the
valley north of the city, reached only
by a narrow roadway or, in later times,
by the Keifuku rail line. Although
the area has witnessed a great deal
of recent growth, it still retains
much of its peaceful character.

Sanzen-in is approached by a
path along a stream leading
past ricefields and an occasional
farmhouse. A flat terrace lined by
curio and refreshment shops on one
side and a handsome stone wall on
the other, is followed by a heavily

三千院　左京区大原来迎院町

planted avenue—a sudden break in the wall admits a run of steps that lead to the temple's entrance gate.

Within the walled grounds of the temple, sits the Hondo, built by the priest Eshin (942–1017), who is generally credited as the founder of the temple. The Hondo was built in 985, rebuilt in 1143, and is called the Ojo-gokuraku-in (Temple of Rebirth in Paradise). Out of the moss that covers much of the ground surface emerge numerous maples and a grove of cryptomeria trees. The straight-trunked cryptomerias branch at a high level and provide a continuous canopy of foliage overhead, creating a colonnade-like space that is both unusual and appealing.

The main garden radiates a calm beauty evident in any season, particularly when it is enjoyed in solitude. There are, in addition, gardens surrounding a building known as the Kyoku-den. A slope supporting numerous sheared shrubs bounds the garden on its eastern side, with the distant Hondo as its focal point.

Comments: Sanzen-in is celebrated for its fall color. The maples become a blaze of color at the peak of their season—usually the latter part of October. Against the green backdrop some trees appear so brilliant in direct sunlight that they seem to be in flames. Autumn brings many visitors to the area, and it is advisable to go early in the day if one wishes to avoid the crowds. In the winter the Ohara district receives considerable snowfall as it is usually colder than Kyoto proper. In the snow Sanzen-in makes an exquisite sight, and one is likely to view the garden beneath its white carpet in solitude.

2

Sanzen-in
1 The garden and Hondo
2 Clipped shrub forms

147

Jakko-in

Sakyo-ku, Ohara, Kusao-cho
Kamakura period, c. 1185
Tendai Buddhism
Hours: 9:00 to 5:00 (March–
November); 9:00 to 4:30 (December–
February)
Photography is permitted.

Jakko-in is a secluded nunnery in
the Ohara district about a half mile
west of Sanzen-in. The temple is
often said to have been founded by
Prince Shotoku in 594, but no reliable
records support this attribution.
Certain, however, is that Kenrei-
mon-in (1155–1213), the widow of
Emperor Takakura, became a nun
and came to live at Jakko-in in 1185.
This famous woman is recorded in
history as the only known Taira
survivor of the battle between the
Taira and Minamoto clans at Dan-
noura, near Shimonoseki, in 1185.

Her clan, the Taira, was also known
as the Heike and the events of
Kenrei-mon-in's life are recorded
in the *Heike Monogatari* (Tales of
the Heike Clan), one of Japan's
most famous historical novels.
Kenrei-mon-in, in time, assumed the
office of head priestess at Jakko-in,
and after her death in 1213 her tomb
was erected near the temple, where
it remains today. While the buildings
date from the Kamakura period,
there have been several alterations
and restorations, one executed in
1603 by order of Toyotomi Hideyori,
the son of Hideyoshi.

The temple precinct is set within
heavily forested surroundings.
On approaching the temple, the
small weathered structures can
be seen among the trees that dot
the grounds. As at Sanzen-in,
the maple trees around Jakko-in
are noted for their fall color.

The main garden is located between
the Hondo (Main Hall) and the
shoin (originally the living quarters
of Kenrei-mon-in). A waterfall
drops in several stages into a small
pond that reflects the green of
the trees encircling it. The area
around this pond incorporates plantings of shaped azaleas, camellias,
pines, cherries, and maples growing
on its perimeter. Some of this vegetation is believed to be quite old,
possibly originating from the temple's
founding.

The small scale of the structures,
teamed with the sloping hillside,
forms an enclosure that with the
diminutive plant and water elements
create a feeling of intimacy. The
mood of the garden is somewhat
bucolic and a bit melancholy—
particularly when one recalls the
sadness associated with Kenrei-mon-
in's residence at Jakko-in.

Comments: Jakko-in, like Sanzen-
in, is very crowded when the
maples are at peak color. One is
advised to come early in the day to
avoid the crowds. The temple is also
a striking sight in the snow.

● 寂光院 左京区大原草生町

Jakko-in: View of garden

Southeast District
Kyoto Key Map

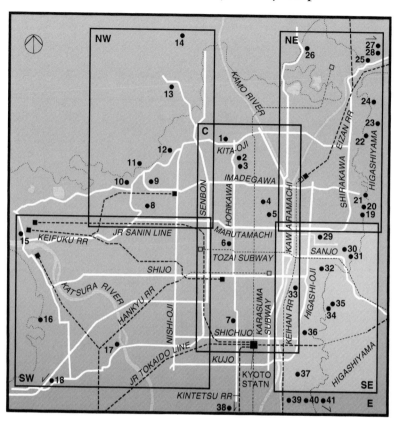

Southeast District Map

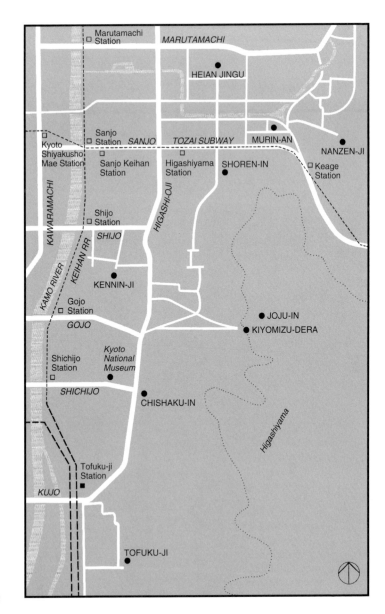

Heian Jingu
Heian Shrine

Sakyo-ku, Okazaki,
Nishitenno-cho
Meiji period, 1895
Shinto

Hours: 8:30 to 5:30 (15 March–31
August); 8:30 to 5:00 (1-14 March;
September–October); 8:30 to 4:30
(November–February)

Photography is permitted.

Special Features: A modern pond
garden that interprets the classical
tradition. Fine cherry blossoms in
spring.

Both the structure and the garden
of the Heian Jingu (Shrine) must
be seen as period pieces of the
Meiji and subsequent modern eras,
and not truly indicative of Heian
design and aesthetics.

In 1892 the city of Kyoto decided to
commemorate the eleven-hundredth
anniversary of the founding of the
Old Capital by constructing a shrine
to honor the spirit of the city's
founder, Emperor Kammu. Three
years later, the shrine was consecrated.
In an attempt to formalize this con-
nection with the past, the most
visible of the shrine buildings were
constructed in the architectural style
of the Heian period, patterned on the
Chodo-in (Hall of State) in the
Daidairi of the old Imperial Palace
compound. The structures were not
realized at full size, however, but only
at about two-thirds of their original
dimensions. Thus the buildings may
be seen as relatively accurate in terms
of style, but much reduced in scale.

The gardens date from the original
construction but were first restored
early in the twentieth century.

The axial symmetry of Heian
planning characterizes the layout
of the shrine, whose dignity is
increased by the extensive gravel
forecourt. To the west, east, and
north, a large garden wraps the
shrine proper in a symbolic recreation of a garden in the Heian style.
Typical of the Heian era, the landscape design centers on a large
pond graced by lavish plantings.
While the design is more the product of the modern era than any
historical period, it is a beautiful
garden nonetheless. Loraine Kuck
points out that the "garden makes

Heian Jingu:
The pond edge and stepping stones

● 平安神宮　左京区岡崎西天王町

153

its appeal because of the plants and trees in it. In this respect it is typically modern [for a Japanese garden]."

The garden of the Heian Shrine is excellent in both details and execution. Ogawa Jihei, its designer, maintained traditional garden concepts while employing new plant materials that entered Japan with the increased foreign contact that characterized the Meiji era. Of particular note is the pleasing progression of features and views, and the sensitive handling of the stepping stones across the pond.

The Taihei-kaku, a bridge in the Chinese style, provides the visual centerpoint. This bridge, which bears some stylistic resemblance to the more noted Golden and Silver Pavilions, effects a graceful linkage between the two shores. Its style also refers to the pavilions-over-the-water, typical of the Heian period.

Comments: While New Year's Day is the best time to see the forecourt and buildings—when they are filled with people in brightly colored kimono (and gray or black business suits)—the garden is best seen in spring, when the cherry blossoms, irises, and azaleas display their full color. A gate on the left side of the court in front of the main buildings provides entry to the garden.

Heian Jingu:
The pond and Taihei-kaku bridge

Murin-an

Sakyo-ku, Nanzen-ji,
Kusagawa-cho
Meiji period, 1896
Hours: 9:00 to 4:30; closed from
29 December to 3 January
Photography is permitted.

Murin-an occupies a site once a part of the extensive holdings of nearby Nanzen-ji. Late in the nineteenth century the temple sold off portions of its vacant lands to members of the upper class and nobles anxious to develop luxurious estates. In 1896 Prince Yamagata Aritomo, a soldier and former prime minister, began construction of Murin-an, its garden, and buildings. Aritomo was a progressive thinker and a member of the so-called "literary" tradition whose thoughts on garden design tended toward the naturalistic rather than the stylized compositions and restricted plant palettes of the classic garden. Though firmly rooted in the Japanese tradition, his garden at Murin-an incorporated new elements such as unusual plant specimens and a grass lawn, adding a new richness without destroying the feeling of harmony.

Although Aritomo is thought to have designed the garden himself, he left its execution to Ogawa Jihei, who also made the garden at the nearby Heian Jingu. Ogawa was born to a long line of gardeners and was well schooled in traditional knowledge. But the era in which he lived and worked—Meiji—was a time of cataclysmic change in Japan, with an impact felt as much in the arts as in technology and political institutions. He found a willing patron in Aritomo who represented a similar fusion of progressive thought and respect for the past.

The garden at Murin-an is relatively small and confined, created by the movement, play, and fall of water from the nearby hills. Streams flow and descend, move through the site, twist through earth and lawn, brush stones, wash pebbles. Tall trees line the boundaries of the site that yields only at a single point to a controlled view of the adjacent Higashiyama. Lawn areas occupy a good portion of the garden, particularly those areas nearest the buildings.

While Murin-an has none of the spectacle of the upper garden at Shugaku-in, or the refined minimalism of the rock garden at Ryoan-ji, it is a quiet, representative example of the transitional form of the Meiji period residential garden.

● 無鄰菴　左京区南禅寺草川町

1

2

3

Murin-an
1 The villa
2 The pond
3 The banks of the stream

Nanzen-ji

Sakyo-ku, Nanzen-ji,
Fukuchi-cho
Kamakura period, founded 1290
Headquarters of the Zen-shu (also
called Busshin-shu) sect of Rinzai
Zen Buddhism.

Hours: The grounds of the temple
are always open to the public: the
San-mon Gate is open from 8:40 to
5:00 (March–November) and 8:40
to 4:30 (December–February).

Photography is permitted on the
grounds and in those sub-temples
open to the public.

Nanzen-ji is situated within a pine
forest at the foot of the eastern
hills of Higashiyama. Originally
much larger in extent, the grounds
now cover about twenty-seven
acres and remain one of Kyoto's
major Zen precincts. (See also
Daitoku-ji, Myoshin-ji, and Tofuku-
ji for other Zen temple complexes.)
The temple occupies the former site
of the detached palace of Emperor
Kameyama (1249–1305), who
retired here after his abdication in
1274. In 1290 the priest Mukan
(Busshin-Zenji) converted the
residence into a temple at the
emperor's behest.

There are presently twelve sub-
temples within the precinct; several
contain notable gardens. The temple's
two-story main gate (San-mon) is
an impressive structure and a classic
example of the "gateless gate" of
Zen, whose purpose is more symbolic
than functional. Built in 1628, it is
well known for its association with
the legendary robber Ishikawa
Goemon. A character on the order
of Robin Hood, Goemon supposedly
hid in the gate until his eventual
capture.

Most of the temple buildings
succumbed to fire, like so much of
Kyoto, during the Onin Wars
(1467–1477). A major rebuilding
was carried out in 1611 with the
aid of the first Tokugawa shogun,
Ieyasu. The present layout of
Nanzen-ji is not as clearly discernible
as precincts such as Myoshin-ji and
Daitoku-ji. The main gate and
prayer hall do align on axis, but
the present structures do not
cohere as strongly as in earlier
times. Nanzen-ji's three most
important temple gardens are open
to the public, while other sub-temples
that possess gardens of interest
require special permission for
entrance.

●

南禅寺　左京区南禅寺福地町

157

Nanzen-ji Hojo
Superior's Quarters

Edo period, rebuilt in 1611;
garden is later

Hours: 8:40 to 5:00 (March–
November); 8:40 to 4:30 (December–
February)

Photography is permitted.

The Hojo comprises two main
buildings, the larger having
once been the Seiryoden of the
Imperial Palace, donated to the temple
at the time of the 1611 reconstruction. The smaller quarters were
formerly a part of Hideyoshi's
Fushimi Momoyama Castle. Both
structures house well-known paintings of the Kano school. The noted
garden designer Nakane Kinsaku
was responsible for refurbishing the
garden about thirty years ago.

The principal garden, of the *kare-
sansui* Zen type, features a large
rectangle of white sand set south of
the Hojo. From the veranda, a narrow
strip of rocks and plantings in front
of the enclosing wall attracts the
eye across the raked sand. Above
the wall, roofs of the temple's structures rise to various levels and make
a striking composition sandwiched
between the distant forest and the
garden's rocks and planting. Several
of the rocks are quite sizable but
through time they have merged with
the foliage of the well-maintained
vegetation.

Like Ryoan-ji, several names have
been poetically assigned to this

garden, including the "leaping tiger,"
derived, it is said, from the form of
the main rock groupings. The signif-
icance of the garden's harmonious
composition, while given many
explanations, is lost to us today. It
would appear that the garden utilized
the traditional dry Zen manner,
although the large stones and their
positioning within the vegetation
seem almost cumbersome when
compared with the refined Zen
gardens of the earlier Muromachi
and Momoyama periods—like
those seen at Daitoku-ji or Ryoan-ji.

The primary attribute of the garden
is its composition of elements set
in space: the sheet of sand leading to
the receding planes of rocks, plants,
wall, roofs, and distant landscape.
Together, they form an impressive
whole that induces the contemplative
state long associated with Zen. This
balanced siting of the buildings and
garden against the backdrop of the
forested hills also contributes to this
garden setting appreciated throughout
Japan.

1

2

3

Nanzen-ji Hojo
1 The dry garden looking west
2 The dry garden
3 Gravel-plants-rocks-wall

Konchi-in

Edo Period, 1632
Hours: 8:30 to 5:00 (March–November); 8:30 to 4:30 (December–February)
Photography is permitted.

The dry garden of Konchi-in is less well known than that of the Nanzen-ji Hojo, although among landscape architects and garden aficionados, it is considered to be historically more significant. Konchi-in is one of the select few gardens that can be attributed with certainty to Kobori Enshu (1579–1647), one of the best-known Japanese garden designers. The eminent priest Suden, the Tokugawa intermediary for the shogunate's aid to the nation's temples, used Konchi-in as his Kyoto administrative headquarters. Suden commissioned Enshu to design and execute some new gardens at Konchi-in, including the dry garden south of the Hojo.

Basically a flat rectangle of sand, the dry garden is bounded on one side by a temple building and on the west end by a small chapel dedicated to Suden. A bank on the opposite (south) side of the building slopes gently uphill, heavily planted with trees and clipped shrubs, and serves as a green backdrop for the garden. Two large groupings of rocks occupy the space before the

1

plantings. The character of the grouping on the right is vertical; on the left it is decidedly horizontal. The dominant visual feature of the left-hand group is a flat rectangular stone set barely above grade in a bed of small stones.

These two rock groupings have traditionally been categorized as the crane and tortoise type (*tsuru-kame*). Since ancient times, these animals have been associated with longevity, beauty, and eternal youth; they have long been used in gardens, particularly those of the samurai or warrior class. It was not surprising that in this unsure and often turbulent world, the warrior aspired to the immortality symbolized by the crane and tortoise.

Both Suden and Enshu were of the samurai class and were certainly familiar with this theme. But equal in importance with the symbolic aspects are the compositional bold-ness and originality associated with the Enshu style. Although softened to some degree by the texture of the foliage, a strong tension devel-ops through the contrast of upright and horizontal planes of the rocks. The clever design techniques one expects from Enshu are also present here, illustrated by such features as the flat stone set on grade and an embankment where one would normally expect a plaster earthen wall. Looking from the veranda across the sea of sand, the large stones among the plants

compose a total landscape scene, perfectly joined, a design reduced to accord with the dimensions of the small temple. The garden perfectly suits its space, and it appears as natural to the eyes as a native landscape.

A pond in the shape of the Japa-nese character for spirit or heart (*kokoro*) serves as the focus of a second garden, east of the Hojo. Containing fine plant specimens and stones, the garden is younger than the dry garden and is not attributed to Enshu. It is more in character with the stroll garden type, such as those at Katsura or Sento Gosho, than those of the dry Zen or medi-tative type.

2

Konchi-in
1 Detail of principal grouping
2 The south garden   161

Nanzen-in

Early Edo period, reconstruction
Hours: 8:40 to 5:00 (March–
November); 8:40 to 4:30 (December–
February)
Photography is permitted.

Nanzen-in occupies the site of a
villa originally built for Emperor
Kameyama in 1274. The garden
has undergone so many alterations
that virtually no trace of the
original remains. The most recent
reconstruction took place in the Edo
period, when the pond and strolling
garden received their definitive
forms. Somewhat deteriorated, the
garden is nevertheless a secluded
and enjoyable locale, its well-worn
character lending it a certain charm.

●

南禅院

左京区南禅寺福地町（南禅寺山内）

162

Shoren-in

Higashiyama-ku, Awata-guchi,
Sanjobo-cho
Muromachi period
Tendai Buddhism
Hours: 9:00 to 5:00
Photography is permitted.
Special Features: Specimen camphor
tree at the entry to the temple.
Kirishima azaleas in the garden
are splendid when in bloom.

Shoren-in temple, often referred to
as the Awata palace, was founded
in the ninth century as a retirement
palace for the emperor and is thought
to have become a temple around
1144. The buildings burned in
1893 and were rebuilt thereafter
in what has been considered a
"Miniature Imperial Palace" style.

The garden was first constructed in
the Muromachi period and is one of
several works attributed to Soami.
It is also believed that the garden on
the eastern side of the building,
called the Soka-den, was planned
by Kobori Enshu. This claim was
disputed, however, by the eminent
garden historian and designer Shigemori Mirei. Shigemori concurred
with the Muromachi origins of the
garden with Soami as designer, but
he believed that the garden was
rebuilt in the Edo period by persons
unknown. According to records, the

青蓮院　東山区粟田口三条坊町

Shoren-in: View of pond and hill

garden was ruined by fire once again in the Meiji period and then rebuilt once more, this time by Ogawa Jihei in 1909.

Obviously the garden has undergone considerable changes since the Muromachi period, no matter who was responsible for them. The scale, for one, is far less grandiose than it was in earlier times. It is, however, a pleasant pond garden with some balanced groupings of rocks and shrubs. Originally intended to be viewed primarily from the verandas of the temple buildings, paths now direct movement within the garden and invite intrusion. In the area known as the "Kirishima garden" are some excellent Kirishima azaleas, which themselves date from the Edo period. A tea garden (*roji*) leads to the teahouse known as Koubun-tei. While this garden is not considered one of the major examples of landscape art, its admirable details and fine plant material reward the visitor.

Comments: This garden is very popular as a setting for *koto* concerts, often held in the evening, and is known to have excellent acoustics as well as a beautiful setting for the music. Check with the temple (Japanese necessary) or with the Kyoto tourist office for information about concerts.

Shoren-in: Detail of hill landscape

Kennin-ji

Higashiyama-ku, Komatsu-cho
Heian period, founded 1202
Rinzai Zen Buddhism

Hours: Grounds of Kennin-ji are open daily: the Hojo is open from 10:00 to 4:00 except over the New Year's holidays. The sub-temples are closed to the public. Permission must be secured in writing in advance.

Photography is permitted.

Today, Kennin-ji seems quiet and sleepy, existing in its own world adjacent to the bustling Kyoto downtown, but from the thirteenth to fifteenth centuries it was one of the most important religious compounds in the country. Established in 1202, Kennin-ji is the oldest Zen temple in Kyoto. Eisai (1141–1215), who introduced the Rinzai sect upon returning to Japan from China, is credited with its founding. The temple flourished under aristocratic patronage and continually increased both the size and number of its buildings.

Having barely escaped ruin during the Onin Wars of the later fifteenth century, the temple met almost complete destruction in 1556. In 1763 many of the structures were again rebuilt, while buildings from temples in other prefectures were moved and re-erected in the capital. Kennin-ji's layout is relatively formal, aligned on a central axis headed by the Hojo, but typical of Zen precincts, this formality applies only to the main architectural core; within the grounds of the sub-temples, little such formal order is evident (see Daitoku-ji).

Two gardens at Kennin-ji interest the visitor: those at the Hojo, or Superior's Quarters; and at the sub-temple of Ryosoku-in. The main, or south, garden of the Hojo is of the *kare-sansui* (dry) type, constructed in the Momoyama period. Enclosed by an earthen tile-capped wall, limited areas of planting play against an expanse of raked sand. The garden appears far simpler in form than those at either Ryoan-ji or the Superior's Quarters at Nanzen-ji and lacks the sense of profundity that characterizes these other two gardens.

The garden of the sub-temple of Ryosoku-in presents quite a different image, showing more influence from the tea aesthetic. Heavily planted to create an intricate set of vistas, the design centers on a pond that links the two areas of the garden. A small hillock distinguishes the south garden, in contrast to the reflective surface of the pond to the north. Two teahouses serve less as focal points for the composition than as backdrops or limits to the garden. Perhaps the garden is better seen *from* the teahouses looking back toward the temple buildings.

●

建仁寺　東山区大和大路通四条下ル

Kiyomizu-dera

Higashiyama-ku, Kiyomizu,
1-chome
Nara period, 637–748;
rebuilt 1633
Hosso Buddhism
Hours: 6:00 to 6:00
Photography is permitted.

Like a huge ship stranded on a mountaintop, the massive roof of Kiyomizu-dera hovers above the mountain ridge, borne aloft by an elaborate superstructure of gigantic wooden columns and beams. The temple's architecture is itself of considerable historical interest, and the Kiyomizu complex superbly represents the latter stage of Japanese spatial planning termed "sophisticated order."

Approaching the complex through the adjacent Kiyomizu district, and walking its narrow curving streets, one perceives little order to the layout. Suddenly a gate and the top of a pagoda appear. The inter-

清水寺　東山区清水一丁目

1

relationship of the temple's many parts avoids ready apprehension—there seem to be many paths and entries that suggest alternate routes. Yet in actuality, every element has been carefully adjusted to create a dynamic spatial composition that unfolds through movement and time. The rigid formality of geometric arrangment has been left centuries behind, and instead, the uncontrived appearance and incremental growth of nature prevails. At Kiyomizu-dera the relationship of all the parts—the paths, the building elements, the upper and lower levels, the balance of constructed and natural—work together to create a masterpiece of spatial and formal composition.

2

Kiyomizu-dera
1 View across the valley
2 The temple perched on its superstructure

167

Joju-in ■

Higashiyama-ku, Kiyomizu,
1-chome
Early Edo period, c. 1629
Hosso Buddhism
Hours: Not open to the general public
except twice a year in the spring and
the fall. Special permission from the
temple is required for entry at all
other times.
Photography is not permitted.
Special Features: A plant, stone,
and pond garden that incorporates
"borrowed scenery" across the
Yuya valley.

The Joju-in serves as the headquarters and priests' residence for
Kiyomizu-dera, one of the most
popular and famous sights in
Kyoto. The temple's situation and
buildings form an intriguingly
dramatic setting that attracts
throngs of visitors daily. Yet very
few of these sightseers know that
tucked just north of the temple's
main buildings lies Joju-in, whose
serene character differs markedly
from the temple's crowded platform.

The north-facing garden shelters a
pool of dark reflective water and
extensive planting, and is best
viewed from the veranda and rooms
of the north *shoin*. Although quite
small in area, the garden expertly
employs the device of "borrowed
scenery" (*shakkei*) to conjure a
feeling of appreciable spaciousness.
While generally attributed to Soami,
with reconstruction work by Kobori

Enshu, little factual evidence supports either claim.

Nevertheless, Joju-in does possess
many of the unique design features
of this period and displays the influence of the Enshu style. The naming
of garden elements to evoke elegant
images in the viewer's mind is one
of these practices. The island within
the pond, for example, features a large
stone called "Eboshi-ishi"—named for
the *eboshi*, a type of formal head-
wear worn by the ancient nobles and
Shinto priests—whose form the stone
resembles. The stone water basin
adjacent to the veranda is known as
"Furisode" to suggest the long sleeves
of a young girl's kimono. In addition to these more poetically named
features, the garden contains numerous groupings of rocks and finely
clipped shrubs, all deftly composed.

The diminutive size of the garden
is visually expanded in two ways.
The first derives from carefully inte-
grating sheared shrubs with natural
vegetation as they step up the hillside
to the north. Farther from the central
garden the shrubs are left less shaped,
encouraging the garden to merge
with the natural landscape to insin-
uate greater depth and limitless space.

The second aspect relies on the use
of borrowed scenery. Looking north
across the garden, the lantern called
"Kagero" (Dragonfly) shares the
garden's center with the "Eboshi-ishi."
Behind the lantern a double-layered
hedge marks the actual edge of the

Joju-in
1 The pond and the "Eboshi-ishi"
2 Stone lanterns reinforce the *shakkei*

169

garden. Beyond the hedge the garden drops sharply into the Yuya valley, with a wooded hill rising on the opposite side. On the side of this hill facing Joju-in, a niche cut from the foliage gently ensconces a second lantern, deftly positioned to echo its sibling within the garden. While the scene may have been sufficiently beautiful without reinforcement, the composition now provides a recognizable focal point and implies that the distant landscape is part of the temple's garden. Hedges mask the valley, disguising the edge, while the formal relationship between the near and distant lanterns perceptually merges the areas and greatly enhances the sense of distance.

Comments: The pairing of two lanterns is only one way of borrowing the landscape, and one of the most contrived. Other manners and devices used for this purpose are described in the entries for Entsu-ji and Shugaku-in. While these *shakkei* gardens differed in technique and styles, their intent was always the same: to incorporate distant scenery as if a part of the garden. Joju-in is a classic and convincing use of this technique.

Joju-in: The garden seen from the veranda

Chishaku-in

Higashiyama-ku,
Higashikawara-cho
Momoyama period, c. 1598
Headquarters of the Chizan
school of Shingon Buddhism
Hours: 9:00 to 4:30
Photography is permitted.
Special Features: Flowering azaleas
in late May.

Chishaku-in was originally founded
in Kii province (now Wakayama
prefecture), but was moved to its
present site by Tokugawa Ieyasu in
1598 as part of Shoun-ji temple.
The garden is attributed to the
great tea master Sen no Rikyu
(1522–1591), although conclusive
proof is lacking. Rebuilt in 1674
by the priest Sosei, the garden and
most of the temple buildings were
destroyed by fire again in 1947.
Some of the buildings have since
been rebuilt, and while the garden
is merely "a vestige of its former
glory," it nevertheless possesses a
certain aesthetic value.

The main garden lies to the east
of the *shoin*. A pond runs the length

●
智
積
院

東
山
区
東
山
七
条

Chishaku-in: View from the veranda

of the veranda, the prime spot for viewing the garden. In the Edo period, the pond was extended beneath the veranda, affording the pleasant effect of placing the seated visitor directly over the water. Looking across the pond one sees a small hill with skillfully composed rock arrangements and clipped shrubs and trees carefully merged with the background trees to enlarge the feeling of space. Azaleas bloom in April and May and make a colorful show against the green hillside backdrop.

Comments: While Chishaku-in is primarily a pond-viewing garden intended to be viewed from the veranda and east-facing rooms of the temple, one should also move to a point where the pond meeting the rocks under the veranda are visible. This merger of structure and water represents a unique and very impressive resolution of a difficult design situation.

1

2

Chishaku-in
1 The hillside and waterfall
2 Hillside of rocks and sheared forms

Tofuku-ji

Higashiyama-ku, Honmachi,
15-chome
Kamakura period, founded 1236
Headquarters of the Tofuku-ji
school of Rinzai Zen Buddhism
Hours: Grounds open all day.
Photography is permitted.

Tofuku-ji, sited on spacious
grounds at the southeast edge of
Kyoto, together with Daitoku-ji
and Myoshin-ji, was one of the
leading Zen precincts in the capital.
At its peak, the temple was considered by many to be the city's premier
religious complex. Even today we
can see the engaging remnants of
this great religious compound,
which has suffered the ravages of
time, repeated fires, and sporadic
warfare. While not as rich in architecture and gardens as Zen complexes like Daitoku-ji, Tofuku-ji
still offers the visitor many features
of aesthetic value.

Three gardens of interest represent
the contributions of three distinct
periods. Two, however, have been
remade in the twentieth century by
the noted garden designer Shigemori
Mirei and are thus more the products of the twentieth century than
of history.

●

東福寺　東山区本町十五丁目

Tofuku-ji Hojo
Superior's Quarters

Showa period, 1938
Hours: 9:00 to 4:00 (December–
October); 8:30 to 4:30 (November)
Photography is permitted.

Unlike Sesshu-in, which is a
modern restoration of a classic
garden, the Hojo garden was a
completely new design realized
in 1939. Because Tofuku-ji dates
from the Kamakura Period, landscape
designer Shigemori Mirei desired
that the new garden should reflect
the simplicity of the thirteenth
century while expressing modern
taste and style.

There are three gardens surrounding
the Hojo, each with a common
character yet distinct vocabulary. At
Sesshu-in the south and east gardens
merge neatly at their junction, but
the Hojo gardens read as separate
events rather than elements of a
continuous flow. Entering the gateway, one first encounters the eastern
side of the south garden, where
stones once used as pillar founda-
tions are now configured as the Big
Dipper. To the left, the tall and
jagged stones of the south garden,
set in a sea of raked gravel, produce
a powerful compositional effect.
The stones are arranged in four
main islands and five mountain
groups; muscular in bulk and thin
in contour, their masses tend to
overwhelm the confines of the space
they occupy. The rippled lines of the
raked sand flow into the western
area of the south garden where

gravel meets moss at the edge of a
low-rising slope. The west garden
consists mainly of low shrubs maintained in a precise checkerboard
pattern meant to recall the rectilinear gridwork of Japanese land division. The checkerboard effect then
softens in the north garden, where it
has been transformed into a field of
square stones set into a carpet of
moss. Thus a consistent geometric
motif informs both gardens, yet
becomes muted in the north where
it merges with a natural gorge at the
garden's edge. This hillside, covered
with Japanese maples, is particularly
beautiful in the fall when the trees
are ablaze with yellows and reds.
The designer has purposely underplayed the features of the garden so
as not to compete with the natural
panorama adjacent to it.

1

東福寺方丈　東山区本町十五丁目

2

3

Tofuku-ji Hojo
1 Checkerboard of clipped shrubs
2 Checkerboard of stones and moss
3 The jagged stones of the dry garden

Kaisan-do (Fumon-in)

Edo period
Hours: 9:00 to 4:00 (December–
October); 8:30 to 4:30 (November)
Photography is permitted.

1

Built in the late 1600s, the garden
of this sub-temple of Tofuku-ji
lies south of the Founder's Hall
(Kaisan-do). One enters the garden
through a roofed gateway and follows a formal stone walkway that
divides the space almost in half.
(This walk was added sometime
around 1877 and drastically altered
the original character of the garden.)
To the west, a precisely raked
checkerboard pattern energizes the
traditional rectangular field of sand.
An area of moss, rocks, and shrubs
anchors one corner of the garden,
its form composed using the crane
and tortoise theme so often found in
Japanese gardens (see Konchi-in).

East of the walk, a pond flows
north and south under a stone bridge,
continuing through a course of
clipped shrubs and rocks. A densely
planted hill rises adjacent to the
pond, enclosing the garden along
its eastern side; structures or walls
bound the remaining sides. The
fragile juxtaposition of the sand
and pond gardens, the intrusive yet
dramatic stone walk, and the green
"wall" that opposes the wood
and plaster walls complete an unusual
and enticing garden ensemble.

● 東福寺開山堂　東山区本町十五丁目

176

2

3

Kaisan-do
1 View of the hillside garden
2 The path divides the garden in two
3 Checkerboard sand patterns

177

Funda-in (Sesshu-in)

Muromachi period, c. 1465;
rebuilt 1939
Hours: 9:00 to 5:00
Photography is permitted.

The garden at Funda-in, also known
as Sesshu-in, is perhaps the most
historically important landscape at
Tofuku-ji. The temple was founded
by Sozan Jozin about 1321 and
first built by Uchitsune Ichijo. The
noted artist Oda Toyo, known as
Sesshu—who lived his childhood in
the western province of Bitchu—
resided at Funda-in when visiting
Kyoto, and he was subsequently
invited to make its garden.

The garden has two interconnected
sectors, one to the south of the
Superior's Quarters and one to
the east. The southern garden
consists of a flat bed of raked sand
and a corresponding field of moss
articulated by trees and hedges.
There are two rock groupings, or
"islands," within the moss: one,
known as the tortoise island, relies
on two levels of stones and features
an unusually shaped rock as its
head. The second island, to the east,
embodies the form of the crane. The
tortoise and the crane, as well as
the pine trees used in the garden,
are traditional symbols of longevity
(see Konchi-in).

The eastern garden relies only on
a plane of moss with rocks and
several trees. The arrangements allude
to Chinese mythology, to Horai,

the Mountain of the Immortals;
there are, as well, small islets in
the form of tortoises or cranes.

It seems that in both sections of the
garden, no real principle of order
prevails, and yet the composition
feels equilibrated. If one looks more
carefully, however, one understands
that a strong compositional order
governs the play of seemingly dis-
parate elements. At either end of
the south garden, for example, two
groups of clipped hedges balance
two islands set between them; an
expanse of sand balances the belt of
moss. A simple two-part order controls the garden: planted against
unplanted, and balance in the verti-
cals of the trees. The dynamic of the
eastern garden, on the other hand,
plays an almost linear arrangement
of rocks against a neutral surface of
moss. Both gardens display a unity
and harmony characteristic of the
finest Zen gardens.

Ruined over the course of time by
fire and disrepair, the south and
east gardens were most recently
restored by Shigemori Mirei in
1939. Thus, the authenticity of the
garden's current form could be
open to question, and more than
one critic has claimed that what
greets the visitor today is more the
creation of Shigemori than Sesshu.

芬陀院 東山区本町十五丁目（東福寺山内）

1

2

Funda-in
1 Shaped plant material
2 The south garden

179

Environs
Kyoto Key Map

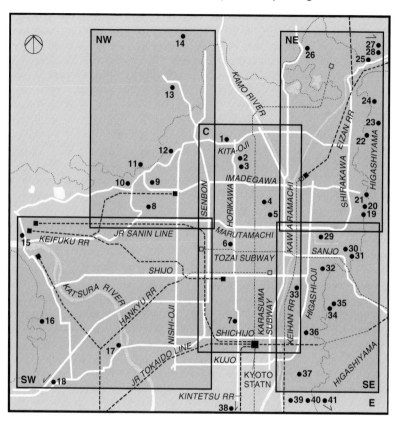

Jonangu (Rakusui-en)

Fushimi-ku, Nakajima,
Tobarikyu-cho
Heian period; garden from
Showa period
Shinto
Hours: 9:00 to 4:30 (last entry 4:00)
Photography is permitted.

● 城南宮楽水苑　伏見区中島鳥羽離宮町

The history of the Jonangu shrine is a long one: its site occupied the center of the expansive retirement villa of Emperor Shirakawa (reign 1073–1086) during the Heian period. Although all the gardens we see at Jonangu are recently made and lack the sense of history that graces so many of Kyoto's gardens, they are consequential in two respects: they demonstrate a respect for, and an attempt to work within, the spirit of historical periods; and they represent aspects of fine contemporary garden making.

The three gardens at Jonangu attempt to represent garden design from three different periods: Heian, Muromachi/Momoyama, and modern. The Heian garden occupies land on the north side of the road, on the same side as the shrine building. The design, in the *shinden* style, was intended to be viewed from the main building of a palace. Two streams, at the northeast and northwest, lead from the pond. An island in the center of the pond, a hill to the east, and a waterfall that flows from the south of the hill, complete the primary inventory of garden features. East of the pond, a "natural" area planted without concern for formal composition, uses plants believed to have been integral to the Heian landscape. Although the total area is small by past imperial standards and the issue of historical re-creation remains questionable, the garden itself—as a garden—is pleasant and well composed.

The modern garden, across the road, is encountered next. High clipped hedges surround a rectangular pool enlivened by fountain jets. There is little of interest here; one feels the intrusion of the new into the old.

Passing from this area one enters the Muromachi/Momoyama garden, like the other gardens at Jonangu, designed by Nakane Kinsaku. This area embraces two sections: a pond and teahouse to the north, and a lawn/rock garden (as it is called in the shrine brochure) to the south. Neither seems to be from either the Muromachi or Momoyama period. Both, however, are beautifully fashioned and well maintained. Thick tea (*macha*) and a sweet are served at the teahouse, offering an opportunity to view the pond and its planting within an architectural frame. A stone bridge divides the pond in two; rockwork and planting convolute and invigorate its shoreline.

Despite the historical references, the lawn/rock garden feels modern in spirit, looks modern in form, and

1

2

Jonangu
1 The Heian pond garden
2 The lawn and rocks of the Muromachi/
Momoyama garden

183

reads as a reinterpretation of such well-known *kare-sansui* gardens as Ryoan-ji and Entsu-ji. But here, the large lawn, itself a modern European influence, replaces raked sand. To the rear, carefully situated hedges screen undesirable elements as best they can. All the elements appear correct, effecting a fine balance between the lawn and the rocks, the clusters of rocks, plants, and the hedges, and the sculpturing of the hedge itself. Of note is the subtle use of the greens of the vegetation played against each other and the blue of the sky.

In all, Jonangu offers the visitor an attractive set of well-designed and well-crafted gardens. Although one can easily take issue with their historical accuracy, there is little point in raising the question: they are, after all, gardens of this century. Good design is coupled here with excellent gardening and maintenance, providing gardens of high quality.

Comments: In spring the drooping cherry trees and azaleas (April) and wisteria (May) bloom, adding a burst of color to the usually green palette. The shrine brochure suggests late afternoon or twilight as the best time for a visit.

Jonangu
Muromachi/Momoyama garden detail

Sambo-in

■

Fushimi-ku, Daigo, Higashioji-cho
Heian period, established 902;
present building and garden,
c. 1589
Shingon Buddhism
Hours: 9:00 to 5:00
(last entry 4:30);
9:00 to 4:00 in winter
(last entry 3:30)
Photography is not permitted.
Special Features: A restless landscape of rocks, plants, and water.
The area is noted for its cherry
blossoms in spring.

Some four miles southeast of Kyoto
proper lie the temple and gardens
of Sambo-in, their history closely
linked to the grand gestures and
extravagant taste of Toyotomi
Hideyoshi. Daigo-ji temple, of
which the Sambo-in is a part, dates
to the Heian period, to the latter
part of the tenth century, although
it found its zenith in the Muromachi period under the patronage
of the Ashikaga shoguns.

The civil wars that racked Kyoto
during the fifteenth century left
little of Daigo-ji's extensive holdings and numerous structures, and
only the elegant pagoda, built in
951, miraculously escaped destruction. By the beginning of the sixteenth century what remained of
the temple had fallen into great
disrepair. Its fate changed drastically when Sambo-in's priest, Giyen,
and the regent Hideyoshi chanced
to meet.

Long known for the beauty of its
cherry trees, the land near the
temple provided the site in 1598
for a blossom-viewing excursion
from nearby Fushimi Momoyama
Castle under the regent's patronage.
Giyen apparently seized the opportunity to request that Hideyoshi
restore the temple to its former glory.
The regent agreed and work began
almost immediately. One story
reports that construction was
completed in six weeks, in time for
a second cherry-blossom-viewing
party.

The garden of Sambo-in links the
austerity of the Muromachi stone
garden with the developed form
of the Edo period stroll garden. It
is a garden filled with richness,
bravado, and an enormous number
of stones. While one cannot really
regard the final product as possessing resolution and harmony, the
composition escapes the merely
vulgar by its brash sense of reck
lessness. There seems to be too
much for the eye to take in at any
one time. The garden eludes a quiet
contemplative regard—some visual
clue, some bit of form, color, or
water always signals the eye to
move on, first to this place and
then to the next. An uneasiness
in the composition urges the eye
to scan, to see, to keep moving.
Although modern visitors are
restricted to the veranda, the garden's
form coaxes them into the garden.
While all the elements achieve
resolution in their way, they are

● 三宝院　伏見区醍醐東大路町（醍醐寺山内）

185

never at rest; the composition feels complete, but this is a restless landscape.

By some counts over seven hundred stones—acquired through purchase, loan, extortion, and out-and-out plunder—appear in the garden. The Fujito stone, the best known, is said to have cost over 5,000 bushels of rice. Yoshiro (Kentei) worked on this garden for almost twenty years, long after the death of Hideyoshi whose order had set the garden on its road to recovery. Over the years each of the stones was positioned and adjusted, balancing the lines and visual forces. The rock arrangement is certainly a masterpiece. Merely *accommodating* that many rocks would in itself be a considerable accomplishment; creating a composition that possesses considerable beauty warrants even greater appreciation.

The Sambo-in garden contains several elements that presage the later stroll garden. These elements are not intended for contemplation, but exist as beautiful and interesting features in their own right. They invite the guest's participation, each view revealed as a series of distinctly separate vistas. A new form of bridge appears here. Unlike the elaborate wooden arched bridges of earlier gardens—clearly constructions in the landscape—simple bridges of natural logs covered with earth form a smooth transition from one path to another.

Much of the material for the garden, and many of the buildings, was derived from other locations. Hideyoshi's short-lived Jurakudai palace provided many of the rocks and some of the plant material—a classic case of adaptive reuse. In fact, at Sambo-in one still senses the opulence of the palace rather than the restraint of the temple.

The later upper garden near the Hondo (Main Hall) employs the double-gourd motif, a symbol of longevity and luck, executed in moss set against a gravel field. Several small gardens fill the courts between the buildings. In all, Sambo-in must be read as a series of spaces, a series of elements, a series of compositions. Its unity is a unity of relationships—one grouping to the next, one view to the next—rather than the singular view of the earlier periods. This is a garden for pleasure, a garden to delight the senses.

2

3

Sambo-in
1 The pond garden
2 The double-gourd motif in the upper garden
3 Island detail

187

Byodo-in

Uji-shi, Uji, Renge
Heian period; Phoenix Hall 1053
Originally Tendai Buddhism, later
Jodo Buddhism
Hours: 8:30 to 5:30 (March–
November); 9:00 to 4:30
(December–February)
Photography is permitted, but not
inside the Phoenix Hall.

Byodo-in occupies the site of the
former villa of Fujiwara Michinaga
(966–1027), in the town of Uji,
which is known for its tea. Michinaga
was kampaku of the imperial court,
thus holder of its highest honor, and
served as intermediary between the
emperor and the court officials.
During the Heian period the Fujiwara
family power reached its zenith; by
clever political intrigue and inter-
marriage with the imperial family,
they held the power behind the
throne for centuries. Fujiwara
Yorimichi (922–1074), eldest son
of Michinaga, succeeded his father
as kampaku, inherited his father's
villa and built the extensive palace
now known as Byodo-in. The
palace was converted to a temple
in 1052. The Phoenix Hall, the
only surviving building of the
complex, was completed in 1053.
Yorimichi retired in 1068, taking
his vows and living out his remaining days within the serene paradisical
setting of the Byodo-in.

The Phoenix Hall (or Ho-o-do),
which served as a chapel to the

Amidha Buddha, is a rare survivor
of Heian period architecture.
Named for the mythological bird
that rises from its own ashes, it is
said that the building's physical
appearance is responsible for its
name: the main hall with its flanking arcades and pavilions creates
the impression of a phoenix either
about to alight or take flight. It
should be noted that the arcades,
or wings, and even the indication
of a second story are purely ornamental and serve no functional
purpose. The building has at times
been derided for this reason, but
visually these appendages serve to
considerably lighten the perceived
mass of the structure. The Phoenix
Hall's imagery provides valuable
insight not only into Heian architectural style, but also into the Japanese
concept of a building as a metaphor. From the earliest times in
Japan, a structure or garden form
might address an architectural use
as well as fulfill a religious or
literary ideal. The entire composition of the garden, in fact, was a
metaphor for Amidha's Western
Paradise—a central image of the
Jodo, or Pure Land, sect of Buddhism.

The building is a beautiful legacy
of the Heian period, and at certain
moments, such as early morning,
it appears almost transcendental,
with its reflection in the pond that
lies in front of it extending its space
and the effect of its horizontal lines.
The pond was once an inlet of the
Uji River and, with the remainder of

平
等
院

宇
治
市
宇
治
蓮
華

the garden, has survived the ravages of time. Although deprived of most of its original elements, this garden with its much-reduced pond still provides a lovely setting for the Phoenix Hall, its primary attraction, and with it displays a valuable example of the Heian environment.

In 2001 the gardens of the Byodo-in were refurbished, purportedly in a closer resemblance to their Heian period forms. A new museum was constructed on the grounds, with a handsome entry court and gardens by landscape architect Miyagi Shun. Visitors now enter the gardens by passing around the rear of the building and exit through the museum.

Byodo-in: The Phoenix Hall and its pond

Joruri-ji

Kyoto-fu, Soraku-gun, Kamo-cho
Heian period; founded c. 1150
Saidai-ji school of Shingon-ritsu
Buddhism
Hours: 9:00 to 5:00
(March–November);
10:00 to 4:00
(December–February)
Photography is permitted.

Away from the infringements of metropolitan Kyoto, Joruri-ji exists within an almost untouched rural setting. Until relatively recently, the large pond and garden in the precinct stood in a state of charming decay, but conditions have improved substantially. The temple itself dates to its twelfth-century founding by the priest Eshin. The long Heian-style Amidha Hall astride the west bank balances the vertical thrust of a three-story pagoda across the pond and appears particularly handsome when seen from across the water.

In 1976, the garden underwent a restoration under the direction of garden expert Mori Osamu. Carefully researching old documents and records concerning the temple, Mori beautifully rehabilitated the pond area to what is believed to be its original character. The present pond is probably no smaller than it was in Heian times, since the steep rounding terrain would have inhibited the construction of a larger pond. It was therefore Mori's task not to alter the garden's features and proportions, but to bring them back to life with the necessary refurbishments and plantings. Thus, banks were regraded, rocks and bridges replaced, shorelines defined, and vegetation added. Of course, it is impossible to say whether the garden is truly representative of its earlier days, but now after several years of aging, the garden provides an informed glimpse of how the temple garden *might* have appeared centuries ago.

Joruri-ji:
The Amidha Hall seen across the pond

● 浄瑠璃寺　相楽郡加茂町西小

Suggested Itineraries

* Permission required from the
Imperial Household Agency.
Apply at your hotel or near the
west gate of the Gosho (Imperial
Palace).

**Permission required from the
temple office, with advance written
application.

Gardens by Features

Index of Architectural Periods

Jomon	4500 B.C.E.–200 B.C.E.
Yayoi	200 B.C.E.–C.E. 200
Kofun	200–552
Asuka	553–644
Nara	645–784
Heian	785–1184
Kamakura	1185–1392
Muromachi	1393–1568
Momoyama	1569–1603
Edo	1603–1867
Meiji	1868–1911
Taisho	1912–1925
Showa	1926–1989
Heisei	1989–

Glossary

cha-no-yu	tea ceremony; the ritual preparation and drinking of tea.
chashitsu	teahouse or room; the setting for the ceremony.
"hide and reveal"	the design concept that restricts views to fragmentary vistas of a garden or building, blocked or diverted by garden or topographic features. Vistas are revealed sequentially, in time, to heighten the effect or exaggerate the sense of space.
hojo	generally, the main building or temple of a Buddhist temple precinct. Often called the Abbot's or Superior's Quarters, it usually includes reception rooms, a memorial chapel, living quarters for the monks, and various service buildings.
ishi-doro	stone lantern; frequently employed in later garden designs.
kare-sansui	dry garden; the presence of water may be suggested or implied through sand, gravel, and rock forms.
karikomi	clipped hedge forms.
kampaku	the highest position in the Imperial court under the emperor during the period from 882 to 1868. The *kampaku* served as intermediary between the emperor and court officials. Toyotomi Hideyoshi (1536–1598), the powerful military ruler of Japan, was given this title

	by the emperor as he was not of proper lineage to receive the title of *shogun*. Usually translated as regent.
ma	the Japanese sense of place; usually regarded as having both a time and space component; space/time.
paradise garden	a garden type that reflects the ideas of the Jodo (Pure Land) sect of Buddhism. The garden is seen as a representation of Amidha's heavenly Western Paradise.
roji	literally the "dewy path." The *roji*, or "tea garden," is the path that leads usually from a garden gate to the entry of the teahouse.
shakkei	"borrowed scenery." The use of a distant vista incorporated as a background in a garden's design.
shinden-zukuri	A style of building layout dating from the Heian period in which a series of pavilions for dwelling, recreation, or state affairs were linked by covered corridors; also the name of the principal building, often flanked by subsidiary structures extending from this central volume.
shin-gyo-so	formal; semiformal; informal. Originally a concept applied to calligraphy, later applied to other arts including the design of gardens. This concept was also used in the design of garden elements such as paths and stepping stones.

shogun	"generalissimo" or "great general." A title given only by the emperor to the leaders of families of proper lineage who ruled Japan. The *shogun*, in effect, held the temporal power in Japan and exercised command in the name of the emperor. Some of the more noted shogunate families and their rule were the: Minamoto (1192–1219), Fujiwara (1220–1252), Ashikaga (1338–1573), Tokugawa (1603–1868).
shoin	an architectural style or building characterized by the low writing desk, from which the style took its name and the raised surface on which it sits.
sukiya	an architectural style characterized by rustic simplicity and extreme elegance, drawing on motifs and materials from rural folk architecture.
torii	simple gateways of varied sizes, traditionally made of wood or stone, that announce the presence of a Shinto shrine. Usually placed at the front of shrines, *torii* demarcate a place of sacredness.

Plants Commonly Used
in Japanese Gardens

Botanical Name (Latin)	English Name	Japanese Name

Trees

Acer palmatum var.	Japanese maple	Momiji
Cercidiphyllum japonicum	Katsura tree	Katsura
Chamaecyparis obtusa	Hinoki cypress	Hinoki
Cinnamomum camphora	Camphor tree	Kusunoki
Cryptomeria japonica	Japanese cryptomeria	Sugi
Ginkgo biloba	Maidenhair tree	Icho
Phyllostachys spp.	Bamboo	Take
Pinus densiflora	Japanese red pine	Akamatsu
Pinus thunbergii	Japanese black pine	Kuromatsu
Pinus pentaphylla	Japanese white pine	Goyomatsu
Prunus spp.	Cherry	Sakura
Prunus mume	Japanese plum (apricot)	Ume
Taxus cuspidata	Japanese yew	Ichii
Zelkova serrata	Japanese zelkova	Keyaki

Shrubs

Akebia quinata	Fiveleaf akebia	Akebi
Aucuba japonica	Japanese aucuba	Aoki
Azalea spp.	Azalea	Tsutsuji
Camellia japonica var.	Japanese camellia	Tsubaki
Camellia sasanqua	Sasanqua camellia	Sazanka
Daphne odora	Winter daphne	Jinchoge
Euonymus japonica	Evergreen euonymus	Masaki
Fatsia japonica	Japanese aralia	Yatsude
Hydrangea spp.	Hydrangea	Ajisai
Nandina domestica	Heavenly bamboo	Nanten
Osmanthus fragrans var.	Sweet osmanthus	Mokusei
Paeonia suffruticosa	Tree peony	Botan
Pieris japonica	Japanese pieris	Asebi
Spiraea thunbergii	Thunberg spiraea	Yukiyanagi
Thea sinensis	Tea	Cha
Ternstroemia japonica		Mokkoku
Wisteria floribunda	Japanese wisteria	Fuji

Suggested Readings

Architecture, Landscape Architecture, and Town Planning

Alex, W. *Japanese Architecture.* New York: Braziller, 1963.

Conder, J. *Landscape Gardening in Japan.* 1893; reprint New York: Dover, 1964, Tokyo: Kodansha International, 2002.

—— *Japanese Gardens for Today.* Rutland, Vermont: Tuttle, 1959

Engel, H. *The Japanese House.* Rutland, Vermont: Tuttle, 1964.

Hayakawa, M. *The Garden Art of Japan.* New York & Tokyo: Weatherhill/Heibonsha, 1973.

Holborn, M. *The Ocean in the Sand.* Boulder, Colorado: Shambala, 1978.

Itoh, T. *The Elegant Japanese House.* New York and Tokyo: Walker/Weatherhill, 1969.

—— *Imperial Gardens of Japan.* New York and Tokyo: Walker/Weatherhill, 1970.

—— *The Japanese Garden.* New Haven: Yale University Press, 1972.

—— *Space and Illusion in the Japanese Garden.* New York & Tokyo: Weatherhill/Tankosha, 1973.

Keane, M. *Japanese Garden Design.* Rutland, Vermont and Tokyo: Tuttle, 1996.

Kuck, L. *The World of the Japanese Garden.* New York and Tokyo: Walker/Weatherhill, 1968.

Kuitert, W. *Themes, Scenes, and Taste in the History of Japanese Garden Art.* Amsterdam: J. C. Gieben, 1988.

Morse, E. *Japanese Homes and Their Surroundings.* 1886; reprint New York: Dover, 1961.

Naito, A. *Katsura, A Princely Retreat.* Tokyo & New York: Kodansha International, 1977.

Nitschke, G. *The Architecture of Japanese Gardens.* Cologne: Taschen, 1991.

Okawa, M. *Edo Architecture: Katsura and Nikko.* Tokyo: Weatherhill/Heibonsha, 1975.

Schaarschmidt-Richter, I., and O. Mori. *Japanese Gardens.* New York: William Morrow, 1979.

Slawson, D. *Secret Teachings of the Art of Japanese Gardens.* Tokyo: Kodansha International, 1987.

Soper, A. *The Art and Architecture of Japan.* Baltimore: Pelican, 1975.

Tange, K. *Katsura: Tradition and Creation in Japanese Architecture.* New Haven: Yale University Press, 1960.

Tange, K. *Ise: Prototype of Japanese Architecture.* Cambridge: M.I.T. Press, 1962.

Treib, M. "Making the Edo Garden." *Landscape,* #1, 1980.

—— "Lessons from the Japanese Garden." *Pacific Horticulture,* Winter, 1991.

—— "Modes of Formality: The Distilled Complexity of Japanese Design." *Landscape Journal,* Spring 1993.

Yoshida, T. *The Japanese House and Garden.* New York: Praeger, 1965.

On Japanese Arts and Related Subjects

Castile, R. *The Way of Tea*. New York & Tokyo: Weatherhill, 1971.

Covell, J. *Zen at Daitoku-ji*. Tokyo & New York: Kodansha International, 1974.

Hall, J. W. *Japan: From Pre-history to Modern Times*. New York: Dell Publishing, 1970.

Morris, I. *The World of the Shining Prince*. Baltimore: Peregrine, 1964.

Mosher, G. *Kyoto: A Contemplative Guide*. Tokyo & New York: Tuttle, 1964.

Murasaki, Lady. *Tale of Genji*. E. Seidensticker, trans. Tokyo & Rutland, Vermont: Tuttle, 1976.

Nakamura, M. *Japanese Arts and the Tea Ceremony*. Tokyo & New York: Heibonsha, 1974.

Okakura, K. *Book of Tea*. 1906, reprint Tokyo & Rutland, Vermont: Tuttle, 1963.

Ponsonby-Fane, R. *Kyoto, The Old Capital of Japan*. Kyoto: Ponsonby Memorial Society, 1956.

Reischauer, E. *Japan: The Story of a Nation*. Tokyo & Rutland, Vermont: Tuttle, 1976.

Rudofsky, B. *The Kimono Mind*. Tokyo & Rutland, Vermont: Tuttle, 1965.

Soseki, M. *Sun at Midnight: Muso Soseki, Poems and Sermons*. San Francisco: North Point Press, 1989.

Suzuki, D. T. *Zen and Japanese Culture*. Princeton, New Jersey: Princeton, 1957.

Suzuki, D. T. *Introduction to Zen Buddhism*. New York: Grove Press, 1964.

Watts, A. *The Way of Zen*. New York: Vintage, 1957.

General Index

The Authors

Marc Treib is Professor of Architecture at the University of California, Berkeley, a practicing designer, and a frequent contributor to architecture, landscape, and design journals. He has held Fulbright, Guggenheim, and Japan Foundation fellowships, as well as an advanced design fellowship at the American Academy in Rome. His books include *Modern Landscape Architecture: A Critical Review* (editor, 1993); *Space Calculated in Seconds: The Philips Pavilion, Le Corbusier and Edgard Varèse* (1997); *Garrett Eckbo: Modern Landscapes for Living* (co-author, 1997); and *The Architecture of Landscape, 1940-60* (editor, 2002).

Ron Herman is a landscape architect specializing in residential and estate gardens, with his office in San Leandro, California. After receiving his degree in landscape architecture from the University of California, Berkeley, he studied the history of Japanese gardens at Kyoto University. He has lectured widely on Japanese landscapes and been the recipient of two Japan Foundation fellowships for garden research. His professional work has been extensively published.

きょうと ていえん
京都庭園ガイド
A Guide to the Gardens of Kyoto

2003 年 10月　第 1 刷発行
2008 年 5 月　第 3 刷発行

著　者　　マーク・トライブ、ロン・ハーマン

発行者　　富田 充

発行所　　講談社インターナショナル株式会社
　　　　　〒 112-8652　東京都文京区音羽 1-17-14
　　　　　電話　03-3944-6493（編集部）
　　　　　　　　03-3944-6492（営業部・業務部）
　　　　　ホームページ　www.kodansha-intl.com

印刷・製本所　大日本印刷株式会社

Kyoto Key Map